D0288487

DIAMOND GOLDFISH

EXCEL UNDER PRESSURE &
THRIVE IN THE GAME OF BUSINESS

Stan Phelps, Travis Carson
&
Tony Cooper

© 2020 by Stan Phelps, Travis Carson, and Tony Cooper

All rights reserved. No part of this work covered by the copyright herein may be reproduced, transmitted, stored or used in any form including but not limited to photocopying, recording, scanning, digitizing, taping, web distribution, information networks, information storage or retrieval systems, except as permitted by Section 107 or 108 of the 1976 Copyright Act, without the prior written permission of the publisher.

Published by 9 INCH Marketing

Editing by Lee Heinrich of Write Way Publishing and layout by Amit Dey

Audiobook recording by Jim Pavett of Allusion Studios. Additional recording and engineering by Scott Bruno of Shotgun Blues Studios.

Interior graphics by Tamee McBee Cooper and Cover Design by Joshua Vaughan of Blue Barn Design Co.

ISBN: 978-1-7326652-7-9

First Printing: 2020
Printed in the United States of America

Copies of *Diamond Goldfish* are available for bulk orders. For further details and special pricing, please e-mail: stan@purplegoldfish.com or call +1.919.360.4702.

This book is dedicated to my oldest son, Thomas Phelps.
Your ability to see the ball and react is one of your greatest strengths.
Always stay focused, work hard, and have fun.

— Stan Phelps

This book is dedicated to my family.
To my wife Alison, you have made everything possible.
To Avery, Ella, Robert, and Ruby - thank you for your love and support.

— Travis Carson

Bee, everything is possible with your love and support.
Men of the Lodge, thank you for always keeping my ego in check, my
heart open & my mind expanding.

— Tony Cooper

ACKNOWLEDGMENTS

We'd like to thank everyone who inspired us, supported us, or provided examples and feedback for the book:

Dave Allgood, Mark Andrews, Barbara Armendariz, Jake Bailey, Bobbie Bauer, Dustin Block, Michael Bowens, Piers Brunner, Faye Bulawin, Sam Calder, Matt Carlson, Dan Casey, Tony Casey, Julian Clayton, Dan Cooper, Luke Dawson, Amit Dey, Tony Elliott, Dave Fano, Amy Favreau, Derek Feinman, Marjorie Gatewood, Mindy Geisser, Adam Gelman, Geralyn Gendreau, Mark Goldfinger, Susanne Goldstein, Shauna Grillo, Kat Hartigan, Jim Hearn, Lee Heinrich, Todd Henderson, Michael Hershfield, Michael Horwitz, Brittany Hurley, Shilpa Joshi, Shawn Kanungo, Karen Kersey, Mike King, Tony Lenamon, John Lewis, Bill Lowman, Jason Lund, Miriam Mark, Tom McCallum, Kyle McCray, Grant McGrail, Tom McDonnell, Aimee Morgan, Steve Mullinax, Erik Munck, Brian Murphy, Jeff Murtaugh, Heather Needham, Samantha Nehra, Liz Nie, Mark Noble, Nikki Pava, Seth Pepper, Carol Perez, Robin Pou, Daniel Ramsey, Jason Ramsey, Kurt Reisig, Craig Robbins, Jennifer Robinson, Luke Robinson, Ben Samuels, Colin Scarlett, Mike Schmidt, Peter Schwartz, Richard Schwartz, Bobbie Jo Seva, Dustin Sheppard, Toshi Shibano, Veresh Sita, Chaz Smith, Michael Smithing, Tricia Sobon, Katherine Steen, Jessica Torres, Tom Triumph, Josh Vaughan, Alberto Valls, Sal Vilardo, Jake Walker, Rich West, and Amy Wu

PRAISE FOR THE DIAMOND RULE

"Do unto others' or 'Treat unto others like you want to be treated' is not good enough to meet consumers' expectations anymore. And the sooner we understand and embrace that, the better off we're going to be. Particularly in this new economy we're in today."

— **Kurt Reisig**

"It is so impactful. Sometimes I'm almost in tears hearing the stories from team members, store managers, and store management about how much it's changed their life because they never had a tool like this before. They never had any exposure to this. They did not understand. They had no vehicle for understanding. It's like you've opened a new world for people. I mean really truly people have been so heartfelt about it."

— **Mindy Geisser**

"First, rather than trying to prepare for any of a thousand styles, I learned I could bucket the world into four styles. Four is manageable; one thousand was not. By learning to ask probing open-ended questions and listening to the answers with an understanding of the Diamond Rule filter, I had a great advantage and insight on what style the prospect or customer on the phone might be, and how they wanted to be treated. And the amazing thing was people would openly declare how they wanted to be treated once you've learned how to listen. It was so easy it felt like cheating! Second, I learned I could replace over-preparation (though a practical amount of preparation still makes sense) by asking the right questions, listening with a Diamond Rule filter, and structuring the call by giving them what they needed. The sales approach is still about acquisitions, but the path of the content is customized on one of only four roads. If you can rely on your new ability to effectively manage the call during the call, you can convert hours of preparation into hours of prospecting. Sales is a numbers game—by using the Diamond Rule I've gained on my number of calls per day as well as improved the outcome of each call. I sometimes feel guilty that I'm either cheating or being a chameleon when I use the Diamond Rule. But the truth is, it can't be cheating when people declare how they'd like to be treated and you give them what they want. The Diamond Rule is simply a tool to help you understand the world and how to give people what they want, which optimizes the chance for us, together, to get what we want—in business and in our personal lives. Pretty damn fine insight."

— Jeff Murtaugh

"I have always felt this weirdness about myself, that there was something different. And there was a certain number of people who didn't like me for some reason, and I could never figure it out. When the Diamond Rule was introduced to me, it opened this world of understanding that people are different. They want to be approached differently. This idea of the Golden Rule and the Diamond Rule, it really just changed everything. It just made sense to me that it's not that they didn't like me, they were just triggered by me. I've done trainings and classes and I never really could understand what my uniqueness was, and I feel like the Diamond Rule gave me that. And it's been very powerful, because I spent many years thinking people just didn't like me. As an "Influence," that was a very hard thing. But now that I can understand what it means to be an Influence and trigger 75 percent of the other people. It just has opened up a whole new world for me, it's been an amazing magical eye-opening experience for me."

— **Bobbie Jo Seva**

"I feel like it's almost the linchpin for my clients. It helps with really understanding who they are as leaders because they often get triggered. They don't understand why they act a certain way, or at least they don't understand why they don't get the results that they want. The Diamond Rule helps me better understand myself and how and why I react the way I do or respond in certain situations—particularly pressure situations—the way I do."

— **Robin Pou**

"I apply the technology on a daily basis. I think it's one of the only forms of coaching that I've ever received that doesn't have an end date. You don't forget it. It leaves a permanent mark on your life. It helps you with your friends, your family, and your business. I would honestly say from the bottom of my heart that the world would be a better place if everybody went through some sort of Diamond Rule training. It just gives you the ability to understand other people's frames of reference and, within that context, you can accelerate action and have a lot more harmony."

— **Brian Murphy**

"Learning about the Diamond Rule has really enhanced my personal relationship so much. I never thought that was going to be a byproduct. I really thought this was going to help me with the people I train and coach. But really, what this turned out to be was a tool that I can use for everything—and especially my own personal relationship with my partner. We have a language now."

— **Susanne Goldstein**

"The Diamond Rule really is a game-changer. The five years that I've spent working in this material, I've grown in it, and I've developed in it. You never stopped growing in it. That's what I love about it. It's not something that you pick up and move on. It really does work. And it really is a career accelerator. It certainly has been for me. I know I wouldn't be where I am today without this material. So I know I'll be continuing to use the Diamond Rule as I move forward in my career."

— **Aimee Morgan**

CONTENTS

FOREWORD

BY

ANTHONY IANNARINO

"There is no more B2B or B2C. It's only H2H: human to human."

- Bryan Kramer

As someone who has spent his life in sales, I have always searched for frameworks that would allow me to see something that others missed, to gain a deeper understanding of individuals and groups of people that make up the stakeholders in any business. The concepts that make up a framework can provide you with insights that literally make the game move slower for the person who can effectively use them. What I have found useful are practical and tactical models that I can immediately apply. The book you are about to read, *Diamond Goldfish,* easily meets that criteria.

Of all the things people tend to resist, selling is often found on the top of that list, somewhere close to public speaking. What many people misunderstand about selling is that it is not something you are doing to someone, but something you are doing for someone and with someone. It is the act of creating value for someone, helping them to obtain a result they couldn't easily create without your help. When you understand this truth about sales, selling becomes a lot easier. But you will have to do the work Stan, Travis, and Tony have laid out in this book.

PRESSURE, YOUR FEARS, AND THEIR FEAR

If you work in sales, you have the pressure of reaching your goals or quota, scheduling meetings with prospective clients, and taking care of your existing clients. You get the added bonus pressure of having your success officially measured at the end of each quarter—and losing deals you believed you would win. That pressure creates a biological response, which you will gain control of after reading this book.

Now, put yourself in your client or prospect's shoes. They are struggling to produce the results they're responsible for creating. They don't really know why they can't achieve the results that used to be possible for them, let alone the better results their company demands of them. They feel a very similar pressure to yours.

The way to eliminate your fears is to eliminate your client's and prospect's fears. Empathy is often expressed as "walking a mile in another person's shoes." While empathy is important, compassion is even more powerful. Compassion is recognizing the other person's shoes are three sizes too small and helping them into a pair of shoes that fit them.

A NEW PAIR OF SHOES

In a clever, practical, tactical, and biological (yes, biological) framework, *Diamond Goldfish* will help you to recognize four different types of stakeholders you meet with when you are selling. You'll also discover their primary response to pressure, as well as how to best resolve their concerns, something I believe is critical to how one needs to effectively sell and serve their clients. What you might have once described as an "objection," is more accurately described and effectively treated when you recognize that it is a genuine concern.

The strategies you learn for working with the four types of stakeholders will allow you to successfully resolve their concerns and give you an unfair advantage. As Stan, Travis, and Tony write early in *Diamond Goldfish*, it's not like seeing the tennis ball spin, rather, it is seeing the seams.

When you recognize who people are and what they need from you, you create the trust that allows you to provide advice. Your deeper understanding also creates a preference to buy from and work with you. It creates a sense of intimacy, that you understand who your clients are, what they really need, and how best to help them.

AN OTHER-ORIENTATION

In my first book, *The Only Sales Guide You'll Ever Need*, my editor smashed two chapters together. One was called Empathy and the other Emotional Intelligence. *Diamond Goldfish* is going to help you identify your style, as well as your clients, an exercise that I would call the key to emotional intelligence.

There are plenty of sales books designed to help you learn to prospect more effectively, to gain commitments, or to ask effective questions. Very few will even touch the idea that your emotional intelligence is a large variable when it comes to success in sales. Even fewer will address your need to be other-oriented, to focus on developing trust and sincerity with such strong advice and direction.

We live in a time when businesses are pushing to be more trans-actional by leveraging technology and minimizing the high costs of managing relationships, in many cases endeavoring to automate that which cannot—or should not—be automated. From my view, all things being equal, relationships win. Even when all things are equal, relationships still win. If you want to make all things unequal, and improve your ability to sell and serve in way that is inline with your values, follow the advice and use the game-changing model you'll find in *Diamond Goldfish*.

— Anthony Iannarino
Best-Selling Author of *The Only Sales Guide You'll Ever Need,*
Eat Their Lunch, and *The Lost Art of Closing*

PROLOGUE

BY

TONY COOPER

The most difficult part of this book project came unexpectantly at the end when we attempted to land on the perfect subtitle for the cover. After all, people always judge a book by its cover even though we're repeatedly told not to. The problem we encountered may not be what you think, however. As a group of opinionated creatives, we experienced no lack of subtitle ideas. In fact, we were easily able to brainstorm a number of really good options. But narrowing them down to a single choice proved much more difficult than we had anticipated. As you might expect, the author of each subtitle was quite fond of their own suggestion and was more than happy to explain to the rest of us why theirs was the right choice. That got us nowhere, so we reverted to the court of public opinion and asked about 100 of our friends and colleagues to weigh in on it. And, things didn't get any easier, which we'll cover in just a bit.

Once it hit us what was going on here, it was hard not to chuckle at ourselves. You see we got caught in the exact predicament that we explain in this book. The "shaking our heads" moment was that we had predicted this breakdown, but still somehow didn't see it coming. See, the premise of this book is that all humans are wired differently. That we all have conversations going on in our heads at all times about how the world is, and how the world should be. We all have strong ideas about things, and we are all pretty certain that the way we see them is the right way. In other words, we all interact with the same world, but we all somehow find it possible to experience it in our own unique way. This is what makes humans simultaneously fascinating and frustrating.

The point of this book is to help you more easily navigate through this complex world of human perception. To understand that the way people see the world *is* how the world actually appears to them, regardless of how that may be different for you or anyone else. When you understand that what's critically important to one person may not even show up on the radar of another, you begin to understand the struggle associated with building powerful and productive relationships, which is what we intend for you to get really good at as a result of reading this book.

Quality relationships are the key to successful business development, and when we are able to produce valuable solutions for others, allowing them to solve real problems and challenges that they are experiencing, our sales efforts become much more successful (and gratifying). But, when we don't know how people are experiencing the world, what concerns they have, what triggers them, and ultimately what might relieve pressure for them, we are stuck delivering the same one-size-fits-all approach that really only works for us. And, this greatly hinders our ability to create valuable relationships.

As you learn about the Diamond Rule in this book, you will see that step one to building powerful relationships with others is the ability to relieve pressure for yourself. When you are able to, what we call, "manage your own biology" in moments of stress or in difficult situations, you can avoid falling into the evolutionary centrifuge that isolates only your self-interest for preservation, keeping you at odds with those around you.

When you can keep your wits about you in those pressure-filled moments, you are able to take the attention off yourself. Only then can you begin to notice that other people have different needs and concerns than you do, and you can orient your approach to specifically help them "manage their biology." Doing so allows you to play at the highest level in the game of business, providing extraordinary value, which in turn grows your reputation in the minds of others. This is the greatest advantage that exists in the game of business. This is playing at the 4.0 level.

When you fully put the Diamond Rule into practice, one of the first things that becomes really clear is that different people want different things in different situations. This can be really frustrating at first because the approach you take with one person just won't work with another. The truth is, you can't be all things to all people, at least not at the same time. And, any approach you take at any time will only work for some of the people you are trying to reach. Truth is, even with the Diamond Rule, you're going to be wrong a lot, but without the Diamond Rule, you'll be wrong most of the time.

So, to help you navigate through this dilemma more successfully, we have simplified the universe of human complexity down to four primary categories of behavior, organized by people's biologically-driven survival instincts. Yes, we're talking about the "fight or flight" response, and it plays a far more prominent role in the game of business than you might think, or that you might be proud of. In this book, we provide you with a map for how each of these Styles behaves under pressure, what feels like pressure to each, what each Style looks like under pressure, and of course, how to help relieve that pressure so you can drive more trust into your relationships and get busy closing a lot more deals.

So, back to the poll we conducted hoping to solve our subtitle situation . . . We presented our assembled group with three options and asked them to weigh in on which they preferred, thinking that the "right subtitle" would become perfectly obvious to everyone, which of course didn't happen at all. The final tally was 31 votes for #1,

35 votes for #2 and 31 votes for #3, a virtual 3-way tie, all statistically within several percentage points of each other. The respondents were completely adamant they were right about their vote, and happy to express their disapproval about the other choices in complete contrast to other people's opinions. We even received 11 votes for a fourth option that we didn't even present, meaning people shared their own suggestions for what they thought the actual subtitle should be!

Like we said earlier, things didn't get any easier as a result of this exercise. This turned out to be such a perfect example of the fact that you can't be all things to all people and you can't please everybody. But you still must proceed.

So, we compiled the useful feedback we received and finalized the subtitle to the one you now see on the cover of this book. So, if you bought this book because the subtitle really spoke to you, we're so happy we hit the mark with you. If you bought this book in spite of how the subtitle sounded to you, we really appreciate looking past that, and believe us, we have other options you would have loved. And, if you didn't even notice that there's a subtitle on the cover, then we feel absolutely foolish for spending as much time as we did anguishing about this decision.

The important part is that you picked up this book and started reading it, putting you on the path to achieving greater prosperity in your life, for yourself, and for others. Prosperity is a state of surplus, a condition of abundance, equal parts wisdom and wealth, where you are able to generate more than you need, making things better for everyone around you. From that place you automatically feel less pressure which allows you to focus your attention on the needs of others and provide them with valuable support and solutions, strengthening your relationships, and creating more sales opportunities. And, that is playing at the 4.0 level.

INTRODUCTION

BY

STAN PHELPS

*"Notice the small things. The rewards are
inversely proportional."*

— Liz Vassey

In 1985, a 17-year-old Boris Becker rocked the tennis world. The unseeded German bested South African Kevin Curran in four sets to win Wimbledon. The tall (6'3") fiery, red-haired player boasted a cannon for a serve. Nicknamed Boom-Boom, he became the youngest man ever to win a Grand Slam title.

One year later, Andre Agassi would also, like Becker, quit school in the 10th grade to play tennis professionally. In the summer of 1986, Agassi would make his splash in men's tennis. The 5'10" Las Vegas native brought a lethal forehand, rockstar hair, and a flamboyant fashion style that turned heads. Within 18 months, Agassi would be closing in on a Top 10 ranking.

In 1988 and 1989, Becker and Agassi would meet three times on the court. Each time Becker dominated Agassi, winning easily in straight sets with his powerful serve—a serve Agassi described as "the likes of which the game had never seen before." The third consecutive loss was a 6-1, 6-3 drubbing.

Looking to solve the problem and reverse course, a frustrated Agassi began to watch tapes of Becker.

He paid attention to his serving motion. It paid off as Agassi noticed a small tick. Just before Becker tossed the ball he would stick his tongue out. His tongue would either be in the middle of his lip or the left corner of his mouth. The position of his tongue would indicate where the ball was going. When standing to right and serving to the left deuce court, the tongue in the left corner would indicate a wide serve. His tongue in the middle of his mouth was a serve down the middle or into the body.

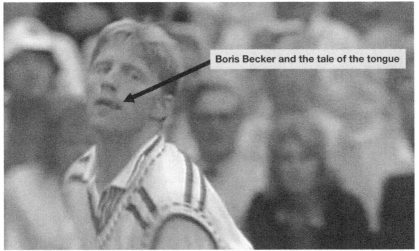

Boris Becker and the tale of the tongue

Photo Credit: YouTube

Agassi would use this insight in his next match against Becker just four months later in Indian Wells, California. It worked brilliantly. He beat Becker handily 6-4, 6-1 in the semifinals.

This small insight allowed Andre to react faster and position himself in the right place at critical pressure-filled points in the match. According to Agassi, "the hardest part wasn't returning his serve . . . the hardest part was not letting him know that I knew this . . . I would choose the moments where I would use that information on a given point to execute a shot that would break the match wide open."

Over the next nine years, the pair would square off another 10 times. Agassi would win nine of those 10 matches.

Tennis, like the world of sales and managing relationships, is about problem solving.

Seeing the little things can make a huge difference. Agassi shared in an interview[1] with *Unscriptd*, "You can't problem solve unless you have the ability or the empathy to perceive all that's around you. The more you understand what the problem is through other people's lens, the more you can solve for people, in life, and in business."

> Throughout this book, we'll use these shaded callouts to share additional background, a quote, or a real-life story. Here's an additional story about Andre Agassi. When Becker had retired, Agassi took him out for a beer at Octoberfest in Munich. He told him about "reading his tongue." According to Agassi, "[Becker] literally fell off his chair. He told me, 'I used to go home all the time and just tell my wife—it's like he reads my mind.'

The Agassi/Becker story is an apt metaphor for this book. If you can see business through a new lens as the ultimate game, you can wire yourself for winning. In the words of Marcel Proust, "The voyage of discovery is not in seeking new landscapes, but in having new eyes." *Diamond Goldfish* challenges you to see sales and the process of developing relationships in a new way. It will provide you with a

---

complete business execution system for generating prosperity and winning in business.

This business execution system is called Market Force®. Market Force is a scientifically-based system with proven effectiveness in the marketplace for over four decades. It is used by leading brands. A partial client list includes Starbucks, Colliers International, Microsoft, WeWork, Alaska Airlines, CBRE, Emaar, AT&T, Savers, and American Pacific Mortgage. These companies leverage the system and its practical tools to power sales and strengthen key relationships in business.

MEETING TRAVIS AND TONY

Travis Carson is the founder of Market Force Global. I met Travis back in 2009. We shared a common friend in Ted Curtin. Ted had met Travis at the Ironman Triathlon in Lake Placid while they were both competing. Upon learning about Travis's background as a tennis player, a JD/MBA, and a business thought leader, Ted made the introduction to connect us.

Travis and I bonded immediately. I'll never forget the metaphor that Travis used to describe the power of Market Force. He likened the system to looking for seams on a tennis ball as opposed to looking at the ball itself. This would enable a player to more quickly determine the spin coming off of their opponent's racquet. The ability to quickly discern the amount of slice, topspin, or kick was significant. A split-second could be the difference between being on your heels and out of position to stepping in and driving the ball for a winner. Over the next two years, I'd see first-hand the effectiveness of Market Force while working as Executive Vice President at Synergy, an experiential marketing agency. We'd land our biggest account and increase our sales by 125 percent by using the Market Force sales system. Nearly a decade later, Travis and I would reconnect. I would meet Tony Cooper, CEO of Market Force. Tony is an accomplished serial entrepreneur who is passionate about bringing out the best in others. He's adept at simplifying complicated issues which translates in helping others to gain new skills and insights quickly. Soon the three of us, a Control (Tony), an Authority (Travis) and an Infuence (myself) would embark on the first sales/client management book in the Goldfish Series.

Diamond Goldfish uncovers how business is a game. The key to winning in sales is managing relationships and minimizing pressure. Performing at the highest level goes beyond simply treating the prospect the way they prefer to be treated. The book will share how the Diamond Rule beats the Silver Rule, the Golden Rule, and the Platinum Rule—combined. Based on over 150 case studies and the science-backed framework of Market Force, *Diamond Goldfish* provides perspective and tools for winning in the game of business.

The book is broken into four main sections:

Section I outlines the **Why**. Here we explore our metaphor of the Diamond Goldfish. We'll share the reasoning behind the diamond as a metaphor and the symbolism of the goldfish. The section will also explore our human biology, examine the impact of pressure, and uncover the four behavioral styles (Control, Influence, Power, and Authority).

Section II explains the **What**. Here we share the process of leveraging the Diamond Rule. We'll uncover how to M.I.N.E. for diamonds with the four-step process of **M**indset, **I**dentify, **N**eutralize, and **E**mpathize.

Section III showcases the **How**. We explore each stage of the sales process using Market Force principles. First, we'll examine the Big Picture. Then we'll look in turn at setting the foundation, hosting the first meeting, and working the sale. We reveal how to acknowledge success and set-up for the next go-around. We'll finish the section by discussing Diamond Rule Matrix, a quick reference guide to assess how your behavioral style works best with each of the four styles.

Section IV brings us home. The book finishes with five main takeaways.

Ready to jump in and upgrade your humanware? We'll start with the evolution of the Diamond Rule.

Let's go . . .

UPGRADING YOUR HUMANWARE (THE WHY)

CHAPTER 1

WHY A DIAMOND?

"Mistake . . . Assume that everyone is like you, knows what you know, wants what you want."

- Seth Godin

*D*iamond *Goldfish* is the ninth book in the Goldfish series. It follows *Purple Goldfish* (Customer Experience), *Green Goldfish* (Employee Engagement), *Golden Goldfish* (Loyalty), *Blue Goldfish* (Technology), *Red Goldfish* (Purpose), *Pink Goldfish* (Brand Strategy/Differentiation), *Yellow Goldfish* (Happiness), and *Gray Goldfish* (Leadership/Generational Insights).

Why diamond and why a goldfish? Let's start with why a diamond.

We believe a diamond symbolizes the best future approach to achieving prosperity in business. Acting in accordance with the Diamond Rule is the next evolution of managing relationships. It's the 4.0 version of winning in sales and client management.

Let's look at the 1.0, 2.0, and the 3.0 versions for background:

VERSION 1.0 - THE SILVER RULE

The Silver Rule is "**do no harm.**" As stated by Zigong, a disciple of Confucius, in the book *Analects*, "**What I do not wish others to do unto me, I also wish not to do unto others.**"[2] The problem with Silver is that it's not prescriptive. It doesn't tell you how to treat others. It merely shares what not to do. It's foundational and not a bad start. Case in point: Beginning in 2000, Google famously coined "Don't be evil" as part of the company's corporate code of conduct.[3]

1.0 SILVER RULE
"Do no harm"

FOUNDATIONAL

2. https://unpolishedjade.wordpress.com/2009/10/08/analects-5-12-proust-and-snobbishness/
3. https://abc.xyz/investor/other/google-code-of-conduct.html

VERSION 2.0 - THE GOLDEN RULE

Throughout nearly every culture and religion, the Golden Rule has become (no pun intended) the gold standard of human dynamics. The Golden Rule is simply "**treating others the way you would like to be treated**." From a moral perspective, this approach seems reasonable, even admirable, and can represent the baseline perspective for raising and teaching children (for example).

If the Silver Rule deals with what not to do, the Golden Rule broadens it to all situations. With the founding of Alphabet in 2015, Google revised its motto of "Don't be evil" to "Do the right thing—follow the law, act honorably, and treat each other with respect." This approach by Google is more aligned with the Golden Rule. Marriott has even developed an entire advertising campaign around the Golden Rule as of the release of this book.[4]

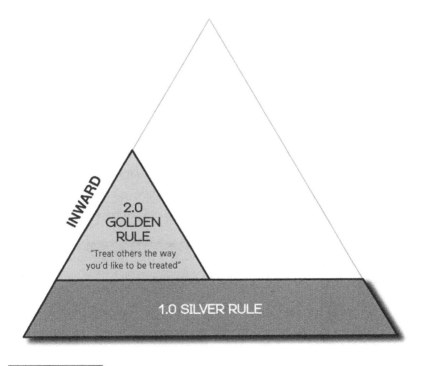

4. https://www.ispot.tv/ad/w6rw/marriott-human-the-golden-rule

Unfortunately, in sales and managing relationships, the Golden Rule a bad rule.

Here's why: In most sales organizations, an acceptable conversion rate is about 25 percent, which means that only one out of every four opportunities converts into a sale. Because you were taught to follow the Golden Rule, it's fair to assume you know what your clients want based on what you would want if you were them. Unfortunately, just looking at the conversion rates tells us that there's an issue. If anything else in our businesses was failing 75 percent of the time, we would immediately look for ways to improve.

The Golden Rule seems to be leading to suboptimal results. This is because not everybody wants the same thing or to be treated the same way. We always assume that if something is good for us, then it must be good for everyone else. And if we want to be treated in a certain way, then that must be how everyone else wants to be treated. Turns out, that assumption couldn't be further from the truth. It leads to failed sales opportunities all the time!

Gold is worth significantly more per ounce than silver. It can be as much as 100 times more valuable. It is also the denser of the two metals, which makes a specified volume of gold worth far more than an equal volume of silver.

VERSION 3.0 - THE PLATINUM RULE

The next level of the Golden Rule was popularized by Dr. Tony Alessandra in 1996.[5] It simply is "**treating others the way that**

5. https://www.amazon.com/dp/B001MSVRZG

they want to be treated." Grounded in emotional intelligence, the Platinum Rule asks you to accommodate the feelings of others.

Dave Kerpen outlines the shortcomings of the Golden Rule in his book *The Art of People*. Kerpen writes, "The Golden Rule, as great as it is, has limitations, since all people and all situations are different. When you follow the Platinum Rule, however, you can be sure you're actually doing what the other person wants to be done and assure yourself of a better outcome."[6]

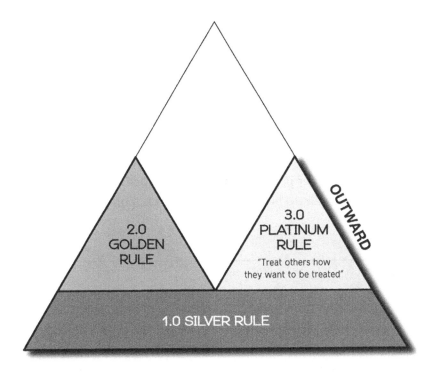

The Platinum Rule is more outward facing in its approach. The focus shifts from "this is what I want, so I'll give everyone the same thing" to "let me first understand what they want . . . and then I'll

6. https://www.amazon.com/Art-People-Simple-Skills-Everything/dp/B01CORLEC4

give it to them." One of the challenges when completely focusing on the other person is that we can overlook how we're feeling and reacting to a situation. For example, we may go into a meeting with the best of intentions to apply the Platinum Rule, but then something happens where we feel upset or disrespected or unheard, and then our capability to actually apply the Platinum Rule is interrupted. Therefore, while the Platinum Rule is aspirational, we must also be true to ourselves and neutralize our biology in order to be capable of addressing the needs of others.

Considered one of the wealthiest Americans of all time, business magnate and philanthropist John D. Rockefeller clearly understood the intrinsic value of the Platinum Rule. He said that "the ability to deal with people is as purchasable a commodity as sugar or coffee and I will pay more for that ability than for any other under the sun."

When you play the game of business by following the Platinum Rule, every game is an away game. You never have the home field advantage because success in the game is filtered through the needs and concerns of the other person. Your playbook focuses only on knowing how others want to be treated and what's important to them.

Platinum is more sought after than gold because it is rarer. Only 160 tons of platinum are mined annually around the world, as opposed to 1,500 tons of gold. Also, platinum is denser than gold; a platinum ring will weigh significantly more than a same-size ring in gold. Platinum is the new symbol of prestige. Think of the "platinum credit card," which often has better benefits and privileges than the "gold card."

VERSION 4.0 - THE DIAMOND RULE

The Diamond Rule takes the Platinum Rule to the next level. It combines the best elements of both Gold and Platinum. Said simply, the Diamond Rule is "**the art of managing yourself under pressure and addressing the needs of others to avoid their triggers**." The key here is understanding both our own biology *as well as that of our prospects/customers.* Treating someone the way they want to be treated is tricky enough under normal circumstances—but what happens when things start to get heated? In the immortal words of former boxing heavyweight champion Mike Tyson, "Everyone has a plan until they get punched in the mouth." Pressure can trigger a biological response that causes us to act in an unpredictable and irrational manner. Under pressure, our brain activates a hard-wired survival strategy every time it detects a perceived threat.

Why is the Diamond Rule so critical in sales and managing relationships?

The answer is simple. A sales situation is inherently full of pressure for both parties. To quote the late artists David Bowie and Freddie Mercury from the song *Under Pressure*, "Pressure pushing down on me. Pressing down on you." Pressure can make things unstable. In sales, you need to manage yourself *and* your prospect/client through these difficult situations.

Rooted in the understanding of our own behavioral style and the styles of others, the Diamond Rule allows you to solve problems and achieve prosperity in the pressure-filled game of business.

Practicing the Diamond Rule requires two elements: 1) you have to see your own predictable behavioral style when pressure hits, and 2) you need the capability to assess prospects/clients relative to four different, predictable behavioral styles based primarily on how people respond biologically to pressure. We'll go into each of the styles in greater detail in later chapters.

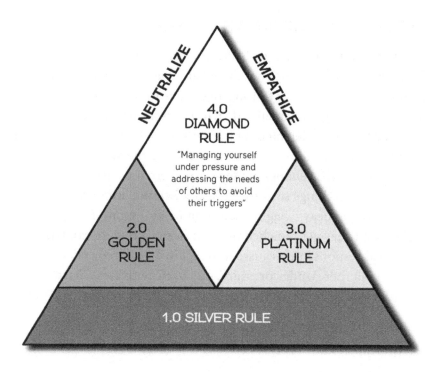

Since we all tend to be pretty strong in only one of the four behavioral styles, it's no surprise that we tend to connect with those
whose style is similar to ours but find ourselves challenged to connect with those who have a different style. Therefore, when working outside of our own category, we may be less effective, leading to
upwards of a 75 percent failure rate in sales conversion.

"A diamond is a chunk of coal that did well under pressure."

— Henry Kissinger

DIAMOND RULE BEHAVIOR

The Diamond Rule is the most advanced approach for working effectively with other people. As a combination of the Golden Rule and the Platinum Rule, it requires you to consider and satisfy your own instinctive concerns and needs while simultaneously addressing the needs of others. Although it takes keen awareness and presence to pull this off, it is truly the "Holy Grail" of human dynamics.

Diamond Rule behavior means effectively managing your identity (personal brand) with others even when your biology (survival

Diamonds are crystals of pure carbon that have formed under a combination of high temperatures and extreme pressure in the Earth's mantle. Diamonds are not found on the Earth's surface, they must be mined with a pick-axe in a tunnel deep in the ground. Given the process of sourcing diamonds and their value, they are much more precious and expensive than gold and platinum combined. CASE(S) IN POINT: It's no coincidence that Diamond Medallion is the highest status on Delta Airlines. Status has four levels: Silver, Gold, Platinum—and Diamond. To achieve Diamond Medallion status (Stan is Diamond Medallion and a Million-Miler with Delta), you must travel 125,000 base miles a year. That's exactly the amount of Gold (50,000) and Platinum (75,000) combined. In the recording industry, the highest level of certification is Diamond. In October 2019, *Old Town Road* by Lil Nas X became the 33rd song to achieve Diamond Certification from the RIAA. Diamond is 10 million units which is 10 times Platinum and 100 times Gold.

response to pressure) is getting triggered (feeling under attack) in the game of business. This is the high-level business relationship game that leads to success. It's rarefied air—diamond-level play. Because rarefied air is high up, there's less pressure. The Diamond Rule allows you to "rise above" and drop the burdens and baggage inherent during high-pressure situations.

When you adhere to the Diamond Rule, you rise above the pressure system, reaching an elevation that makes it easy to focus on solving client problems and reducing the pressure they feel. This makes you stand out as unique and better in the eyes of your client, dramatically increasing your ability to win business.

In this book, our goal is for you to see a Diamond as a symbol of wealth and wisdom. The more you mine for diamonds in your pursuits, the more success you will reap. Unlike Gold or Platinum which can be molded, you need to work with the natural elements of Diamonds and the natural reactions of human biology.

Let's look at the symbolism of a goldfish in the next chapter.

CHAPTER 2

WHY A GOLDFISH?

*"The search for meaningful distinction is central to the
marketing [and sales] effort.
If marketing [or sales] is about anything, it is about
achieving customer-getting distinction by differentiating
what you do and how you operate.
All else is derivative of that and only that."*

—Theodore Levitt

Why a goldfish in *Diamond Goldfish*? The origin of the goldfish as a symbol dates back to 2009 when it became the signature of this book series. The goldfish represents something small that, despite its size, can make a big difference.

For example, Kimpton Hotels are famous for the attention they put on guest experience. The hotel chain has a number of signature additions that go above and beyond expectations. If you stay at a Kimpton, you can count on there being free gourmet coffee and fresh fruit in the lobby 24 hours a day. In the afternoon they host a wine tasting. Not samples—full glasses of specially selected wine. Some Kimpton hotels will let you take out a bike for free to tour the city. All Kimptons are pet-friendly. Bring your dog for free and they'll treat your pup like royalty.

Our favorite little extra was introduced by Kimpton at each Hotel Monaco back in 2001. Perhaps you are staying at a Kimpton and getting a little lonely. Or maybe you and your family are away from home and missing your pet. The little extra is a program called Guppy Love. It offers guests the opportunity to adopt a temporary travel companion—a goldfish—for the duration of their stay. This unique program gained the chain national attention. Steve Pinetti, Senior Vice President of Sales & Marketing for Kimpton Hotels and Restaurants, shared:

> The 'Guppy Love' program is a fun extension of our pet-friendly nature as well as our emphasis on indulging the senses to heighten the travel experience. Everything about Hotel Monaco appeals directly to the senses, and 'Guppy Love' offers one more unique way to relax, indulge, and promote the health of mind, body, and spirit in our home-away-from-home atmosphere.

The symbolism of a goldfish also dates back to Stan's childhood. At age six, his first pet was a goldfish named Oscar. He won it at a fair by throwing a ping pong ball in a carnival game. Oscar was small, maybe an inch in length. It turns out that the average goldfish is just over 3 inches. Yet the longest in the world is just under 20 inches. Not a carp or a koi, but an ordinary goldfish. That's more than six times the average size. The same thing applies to sales. Some salespeople are average, some below average, and some perform at multiples of the average.

Photo Credit: YouTube

FACT

The current Guinness Book of World Records holder for the largest goldfish hails from the Netherlands at a whopping 19 inches (50 centimeters). To put that in perspective, that's about the size of the average domesticated cat.

Six times larger! Imagine walking down the street and bumping into someone who's nearly three stories tall. How can there be such a disparity between your garden-variety goldfish and its monster cousins?

It turns out that the growth of the goldfish is determined by five factors. And those same five factors also relate to the growth of any business and/or salesperson.

LET'S UNPACK THE FIVE FACTORS:

#1. The first growth factor for a goldfish is the **SIZE OF THE EN-VIRONMENT** they are in. The size of the bowl or pond is one determinant of how much they will grow. The size is a direct correlation. The larger the bowl or pond, the larger the goldfish can grow. The smaller the bowl or pond, the lesser the growth. In business, what's the equivalent of the bowl or the pond? It's simply the **MARKET** for your product or service.

Takeaway: The bigger the market, the more you can grow.

#2. The second growth factor for a goldfish is the **NUMBER OF OTHER GOLDFISH** in the environment. This is an inverse correlation. The more goldfish in the bowl or pond, typically the less growth achieved. With fewer goldfish, the more growth opportunity. Who are the other goldfish in business? They are your **COMPETITION.**

Takeaway: The more competition, the harder it is to grow. The less competition, the easier it is to grow.

#3. The third growth factor is the **QUALITY OF THE WATER** that the goldfish is in. Nutrients and cloudiness in the water will impact the growth of a goldfish. The better the quality—the more nutrients and less cloudiness in the water—the more growth. Conversely, fewer nutrients and more cloudiness will hamper growth.

What is the equivalent of the quality of water in business? Here we need to think in a macro and environmental sense. The quality of the water is the **ECONOMY**. It is a direct correlation.

Takeaway: The better the quality of the economy and the greater consumer confidence, the larger the growth. The weaker the economy or capital markets, the more difficult it is to access capital and grow.

#4. The fourth growth factor for a goldfish is how they're treated in the **FIRST 120 DAYS** of life. The nourishment and treatment they receive as babies are keys to future growth. Goldfish are tiny when they are born, usually with about a hundred brothers and sisters. They are about the size of the head of a pin. What do you call a baby goldfish? A baby goldfish is a fry, as in "small fry." The lower the quality of the food and treatment, the more the goldfish will be stunted for future growth. What's the equivalent of the first 120 days in business? A business is typically called a **START-UP** during its early days in business.

FACT

A malnourished goldfish in a crowded, cloudy environment may only grow to 2 inches (5 centimeters).

Takeaway: How a start-up does in the first four months of its existence will be a determining factor of how it will do the long term.

#5. The fifth and final growth factor for a goldfish is **GENETIC MAKEUP**. The strength of its genetics will determine future growth. The stronger its genes and the more it is separated from the rest of the goldfish, the more it typically grows. The poorer the genes and the more it hangs out in the same goldfish group, the less it can grow. What's the equivalent of genetic makeup in business? It is **DIFFERENTIATION**.

Takeaway: The more differentiated the product or service from the competition, the better the chance for growth. The less differentiated and the more a business is like the competition, the harder it will be to grow.

WHICH OF THE FIVE FACTORS CAN YOU CONTROL IN SALES?

Let's assume you have an existing product or service and have been in business for more than four months. Which of the remaining four factors do you have control over?

1. Size of the bowl = Market
2. Number of other goldfish = Competition
3. Quality of water = Economy
4. ~~First 120 Days = Startup~~
5. Genetic makeup = Differentiation

Do you have any control over the market, your competition, or the economy? NO, NO, and NO. The only thing you have control over is your genetic makeup or how you differentiate what you do and how you do it. In sales, how do you stand out in a sea of sameness?

In terms of differentiation, success in sales typically comes down not to your technical expertise but to how you make someone feel. Technical expertise gets you the meeting; the ability to effectively manage the relationship wins you the business.

In summary, the goldfish in *Diamond Goldfish* represents differentiation. How do you stand out by doing the little things that can make a big difference? The diamond symbolizes how well you manage under pressure by upgrading your "humanware" in business.

How can you upgrade your "humanware?" To find the answers, we'll look into human biology and the importance of managing pressure.

CHAPTER 3

BIOLOGY AND PRESSURE

*"Between stimulus and response, there is a space.
In that space is our power to choose our response.
In our response lies our growth and our freedom."*

— Victor Frankl, Austrian neuroscientist and
Holocaust survivor

When selling to or working with other people, there is a lot more going on than you might first imagine. We've all been in situations with "otherwise normal people" who've completely lost their minds for "no good reason."

In fact, there is always a reason for bad behavior, just not necessarily one that makes a whole lot of sense rationally speaking. The picture only becomes clearer when you are able to look under the surface at what is happening to people **biologically**, NOT psychologically.

The field of neuroscience shows us that a large part of human behavior is actually hard-wired into our system through set patterns of neural flow in the brain. Scientists refer to these set patterns as neural pathways. These pathways are like railroad tracks and our thoughts are like rail cars. The tracks ensure that you engage in the same patterns of behavior over and over again. These patterns or "schemas" are vital in order to avoid precious brainpower being spent on otherwise mundane things.

Your brain is the largest consumer of energy in your body. Brain expert Michael Richardson explains that "the brain's primary function—processing and transmitting information through electrical signals—is very, very expensive in terms of energy use." As such, your brain has evolved specific systems to use that energy as conservatively as possible. Unlike other parts of your body, such as muscle groups that can store excess carbohydrates, your brain doesn't have the ability to store energy. Therefore, it must be a highly efficient energy consumer. One of your brain's primary conservation strategies is converting repetitive behaviors and thoughts into habits via neural pathways. In this way, you are able to complete a wide range of tasks and remain productive, essentially without thinking.[7]

---

7. https://www.brainfacts.org/brain-anatomy-and-function/anatomy/2019/how-much-energy-does-the-brain-use-020119

One habit that we all have hard-wired in us is *survival*. These pre-programmed patterns of behavior are designed to save our lives in moments of actual pressure—actual as in real life-or-death situations. When our bodies detect a threat, our biology kicks into high gear to drive a fight or flight response. We respond completely without conscious thought. This is why when people survive a near-death experience, they often struggle to recall what even happened. If we were to draw an image, it would look like this:

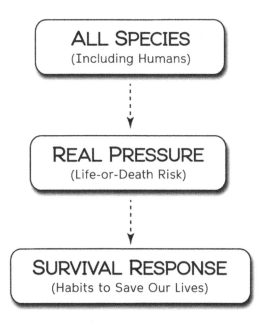

Interestingly, this hard-wired pattern of brain function (designed to save our lives) is more easily triggered than you might think. It turns out that our survival strategies are employed in many situations when there is no actual threat to our lives. This is what leads us to following the Golden Rule under pressure.

This isn't just happening to you; it's also going on in the people around you all the time, including your prospects, your clients, and your colleagues. The way to recognize this is through awareness—awareness of biology that most of us are never taught. Luckily for you, you are about to get a master class on building this sense of awareness. Your new eyes await.

SEEING BEYOND SURVIVAL

One of the primary things separating the human experience from other species on the planet is that we humans have developed an extraordinary capacity to experience multiple types of pressure (or risk) in our lives. In other words, we generally solved our life-or-death issues. Then, as if we got bored or anxious, we invented a game. That game is business. It includes doing projects, selling goods and services, building teams, and running organizations.

We generally characterize the threats that come in the game of business under one umbrella—namely as a risk to our identity. We will discuss this more in a bit, but for now, think of identity risk this way: if a potential opportunity you are working on does not close, we all know intellectually that we won't die.

Take it to the extreme. Say you struggled to close any deals in the next quarter, and you were to get fired. True, getting a new job might be difficult as you look for your next gig—but that's not death. But, *try telling that to your body*. Remember, your body's survival response is a reality of biological wiring, not psychological wiring.

Because other species really only deal with the pressure of threats to their lives, their survival response is perfectly designed to give them the best chance to live. Unfortunately, using our survival response when survival is not at stake is the wrong application for the problem! Consider the following diagram:

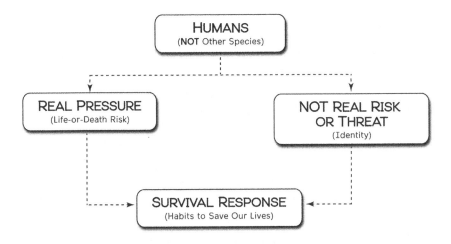

As a side note, this diagram is substantiated by the social evidence that the #1 fear in the world (generally) is the fear of public speaking. Think about that for a minute. We, as humans, have so lost perspective that when asked what we fear the most, we will say identity risk over actual death! In the words of comedian Jerry Seinfeld, "For the average person, if you have to be at a funeral, you would rather be in the casket than doing the eulogy."

Back to the matter at hand . . .

In essence, while we have expanded the number of things that concern us, our method for handling them remains pretty much the same from a hard-wiring perspective. Why? Because our brain has a really hard time distinguishing between actual risk (threat of the loss of our life) and perceived risk (threat of the loss of our identity). Our brains are wired to respond to threats in a particular way—regardless of the actual threat.

This is where neuroscience provides a fascinating explanation of what is going on.

LOSING YOUR MIND

The human brain is the most powerful processor on the planet. It's responsible for incredible advances in art, culture, and technology. Yet at times it can cause us to act like anything but a human being.

Here's how it works. Our brains are comprised of three primary areas. Let's examine each, working from the inside out:

- **Amygdala** - The most primitive part of the brain is called the amygdala. It's about the size of an almond and sits at the base of the brain stem. It is the first part of the brain that forms, and its primary role is to act as a human highlighter—a radar that constantly scans the environment. The amygdala's primary role is to look for anything in our lives that could be a threat to our existence. Fun fact: The amygdala is sometimes referred to as the "lizard brain" because it's the only part of the brain a reptile has.

- **Limbic System** - The amygdala resides inside the wider limbic system, the area of our brain responsible for our basic drive for things such as hunger, sex, dominance, and caring for offspring. It's also the place where we experience emotions, moods, and motivation, and where instinct originates. The limbic system maintains the storage area for our long-term memory. This explains why many of our memories tend to be more emotionally based than factual. Finally, the limbic system helps with bodily functions, such as heart rate, pupil dilation, and the regulation of our sweat glands.

- **Neocortex** - The outermost layer of the brain is the neocortex. It is the largest and most complex part of the human brain. The neocortex is involved with all higher functions such as sensory perception, spatial reasoning, language, and complex thought. It's where things like art, science, and culture live within us. You could argue that the neocortex is the thing that makes us uniquely human. **That is, until the moment we experience pressure.**

When humans are exposed to a high-enough level of pressure—for instance when you find yourself in a tense negotiation with a client—the human brain loses its ability to distinguish between actual and perceived risk. This causes the amygdala to kick into high gear to protect you from an impending (non-life threatening) situation that it fears may kill you.

Put this combination of events together and think about what happens . . .

In this moment of perceived risk, your amygdala senses the threat and lights up your limbic system. The limbic system then triggers your heart to start racing, makes your breath get shallow, or causes you to break out in a sweat. Some permutation of survival begins. Meanwhile, your neocortex is being told by your body: "Hey, take a seat on the sidelines." Again, using public speaking as an example, think about what happens when you stand up in front of a room to speak. Mark Twain made light of this when he said, "There are only two types of speakers in this world. The nervous . . . and the liars."

Remember, this is a biological reaction, not a psychological one. No one would say this is a rational response!

So, while we humans are advanced beings living in a modern world, it turns out we are still operating on fairly primitive biology. And under pressure, that biology predictably runs our hard-wired survival strategy every time it detects a threat.

Awareness creates choices.

OVERCOMING BIOLOGY

If you ever find yourself in a life-or-death situation, you will find that your innate reactions represent your greatest chance for survival. It is in these (hopefully rare) moments when you can truly appreciate the natural wisdom of your behavioral style and its ability to keep you alive.

But, given the relatively infrequent number of times when you find your life at stake, we are suggesting that you are far more than just your biology's reactions to threat. And to effectively apply the Diamond Rule, you must recognize the role that pressure and biology play in your life. The only way to overcome them is through awareness. Awareness will NOT make your biology go away, as it is part of a billion-year-old imperative for survival. Believe us, as long as you're breathing, your biology is not going anywhere, because it has a constant, very important job to do.

Instead, we are suggesting that you learn to behave in ways that are counter to what your biology wants you to do. And do so by making better choices. Applying the Diamond Rule means keeping your wits about you, focusing on the other person, and not succumbing to the pressure. To quote legendary football coach Lou Holtz, "Only the unprepared are overcome by pressure."

A BETTER WAY

Under pressure, we need to leverage our neocortex to control the situation. In other words, we should use the part of our brain that designed the game of business. Use your thinking brain to handle identity risk situations and leverage the right tool in the right situation.

Let's use a diagram to distinguish what we are saying:

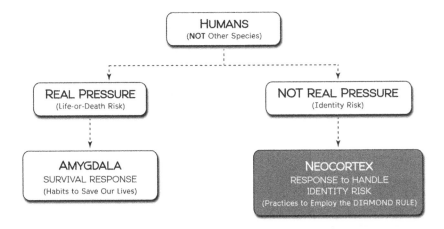

When you develop awareness and really begin to pay attention, you may notice that your survival response is far too easily engaged. However, once you begin to see this pattern in yourself, you can notice it in others—especially when the pressure picks up. When the pressure begins to trigger, you can use that information to dramatically improve your ability to interact and work with others by reducing pressure for them.

"I don't feel pressure in a negative way. I like pressure. I feel excitement and calm at the same time. No pressure, no diamonds."

— Conor McGregor, Mixed Martial Arts Champion

Neuroscience shows that while the primitive survival strategies are hard-wired into your brain, you actually have the ability to lay new pathways over the old ones, altering your behavior. In other words, while your amygdala has no reasoning, it can be reasoned with—you can teach your amygdala not to activate under identity pressure.

By regularly paying attention, intentional repetition allows you to lay down new "train tracks" of hard-wired behavior. This happens slowly, but when our neural pathways and associations change, our brain chemistry also changes. Remember the words of Victor Frankl who said, "Between stimulus and response, there is a space. In that space is our power to choose our response. In our response lies our growth and our freedom."

"Breakdowns in my business became almost a weekly event between me and the other person running the business. Now I understand it was just a style issue. It helped me soothe the situation for myself, knowing that it was somebody's concern, and it wasn't an attack on me personally. Also, I think it helped me be able to acknowledge somebody else's contribution or accomplishment properly. You know it all went back to—this is just a game. It's not personal. No one's trying to hurt each other here."

RECOGNIZING BUSINESS AS A GAME AND SEEING THINGS DIFFERENTLY

The ultimate goal is to become better observers of how we and others respond to pressure. Pressure is the key anchor in the Diamond Goldfish framework. You see, without pressure we are all free to behave in whatever manner we feel is the most appropriate. However, when pressure increases—as it often does in business—we tend to fall into very predictable patterns of behavior. As you become a more skillful observer of these patterns, you can wire yourself for winning. In the words of Marcel Proust: "The voyage of discovery is not seeking new landscapes, but in having new eyes."

Let's focus on the two primary skills you'll need to develop to employ the Diamond Rule:

1. *Learning how to manage your own behavior under pressure*

   Before you will ever be able to relate better to others, it's important to look in the mirror and be able to manage your own reactions to pressure.

2. *Increasing your focus on the concerns of others*

   When you learn what causes other people to feel stress, you can help reduce their pressure and instantly improve your identity along the way.

Improving and combining these two skills will improve your reputation, advance your career, and create success in the game of business.

"It takes 20 years to build a reputation and five minutes to ruin it. If you think about that, you'll do things differently."

— Warren Buffet

WHAT IS PRESSURE IN BUSINESS?

Now that you have seen the brain science and biology behind pressure, the question becomes: "Why does it affect us in business?"

To answer this question, let's look more deeply at the pressure we face as human beings. In prehistoric times, the only types of pressure we faced were life-threatening situations—things like food shortage, lack of protection from the environment, illness and disease, and threatening attacks from animals or other humans. We refer to these situations as "actual" pressure, true life-or-death scenarios. To live through the risk of death required a biological survival response.

Over time, our ancestors sought to create permanent safeguards to these threats. They began to settle down. They started developing their civilizations and cultivating their societies to provide themselves with basic necessities of food, clothing, and shelter. With these needs no longer a constant challenge, survival became much less of a concern.

This caused a dramatic shift in our history as it left the amygdala with a whole lot less to do. As it turns out, the amygdala had no intention of lying down on the job. Given its primitive nature and single-focused survival imperative, all it knows how to do is keep patrolling its environment and scanning for potential threats—even if there aren't any. And it never leaves its post, even when you're sleeping!

It was under these conditions that a whole new type of pressure emerged, which we call "perceived" risk. These are situations that we face every day that feel very, very threatening, but no matter how bad they get, there is no chance of us dying. Typically, at worst, there is humiliation and damage to our reputation if there is a failure. With perceived risk, survival is not at stake.

The irony here is that the safer our lives have gotten, the greater the number of threats the amygdala detects. As the threshold for *what constitutes a threat* gets lower and lower, humans massively began to expand our ability to experience pressure. Humans are the only species on the planet to experience two different types of pressure.

It is this confusion between an actual threat and perceived risk that is the source of so much stress in our lives. You see, business is just a game we invented after we became a civilized species. It is an entertaining and useful game, but when we treat it like it's life-or-death, we suffer.

Now referring to business as "a game" isn't meant to downplay its importance or significance. It's merely to put it into perspective. The game of business comes with real consequences of success and failure. Making mistakes is frustrating, failing to win a project can really sting, and getting fired could be devastating. But regardless of how those things make you feel, none of them will actually kill you. This is what we mean by calling it a game.

The mere fact that we are able to feel this type of pressure so deeply makes it really hard to distinguish between actual and perceived threats. Once your amygdala gets triggered and your biology takes over, there literally is no difference between the two since your brain responds in the exact same way.

If you look at business through your own experience, you will notice that the most successful people in business have figured out that *business is just a game*. These same people have figured out the purpose of the game of business. The purpose of the game is to create, grow, and maintain your identity. When we lose sight of this purpose, we may undertake a number of tasks, but they won't be driving to the goal of building our identity. It would be like playing basketball, but just dribbling non-stop. The purpose of the game is to score. Understanding this key fundamental will change the game in your favor moving forward.

"Business is a game, played for fantastic stakes, and you're in competition with experts. If you want to win, you have to learn to be a master of the game."

— Sidney Sheldon

Let's examine business as a game . . .

First, how do we know that the game of business is not life-or-death? Well, it's simply because even if we fail in business, we don't die! So, we know the game cannot be for our lives. Second, and this surprises many people, the game is not for money. Nope. It turns out the game of business is for "identity." Think about the most successful people you know who create, establish, grow, and manage their identity over time. Those are the ones who win more often in the game.

By way of analogy, think of your identity as a publicly-traded stock. At any point, its share price is based on the collective perception of others of how much it's worth. So, just as a stock price goes up and down over time, your identity does as well. In the case of business, the *measurement* of your identity is the assessment people have about how much value *you create for them* combined with how much they trust you.

That's the formula.

Identity = Value + Trust

When people make the mistake of playing the game of business as if it is life-or-death, they lose the ability to differentiate between "actual pressure" (a threat to their life) and "business pressure" (a threat to their identity). The result of this oversight is that our biology gets involved.

Once that happens, habits begin to kick in to save our lives, *even though nobody is trying to kill us!* Think about that for a minute as it's quite important. And it is just as important for us to know that habits have two observable characteristics:

1. They are repetitive.

2. They are unconscious.

Before we go further, it is crucial that we acknowledge that you, and everyone else in the game of business, engage in both "good" habits and "bad" habits. Simply stated:

- A good habit is something you do that helps you achieve your desired identity and your intended future.

- A bad habit, well, that's the opposite. A bad habit works against your desired future and damages your identity.

Obviously then, the bad habits are the ones you want to eliminate from your game. The first step to changing a habit is to become aware (or conscious) of what you are doing. The moment this happens, you shift the second condition of what constitutes a habit. Through awareness, you can transform what you are doing under pressure from being a habit into being a *choice*.

Once aware, you can activate your neocortex, begin to change your game, and consider the following three questions:

1. Is this how *I want to behave?*

2. Is this how *I want to be seen by others?*

3. Am I *focused on others* at this moment?

If the answer to these three questions is "yes," then keep up the good work. But if you answer "no" to even one, with awareness you can take the initiative to stop acting in that manner. Becoming more aware of your habits—acknowledging and managing your habits in the face of pressure—begins to give you access to applying the Diamond Rule.

In the next chapter let's start this initiative by looking at the four Behaviorial Styles that represent our biological instincts . . .

CHAPTER 4

THE STYLES

"It's not about having the right opportunities.
It's about handling the opportunities right."

— Mark Hunter

Ａt this point, many people begin to wonder why they haven't been aware of how their biology impacts their behavior until now. The quick answer is that you (like most people) made the mistake of confusing your "self" with your amygdala, believing "you" and not your biology are in charge of your behaviors.

Now that you are in your thinking brain (your neocortex), give us a bit of time to show you the differences in the four Behavioral Styles. As you read this chapter, be thinking: "Which Style is most like me?" Honestly, that's the price of admission. There is no rank order, no best Style, none of that! Just by knowing what your default is, you can overcome it and begin applying the Diamond Rule to your relationships.

PERSONAS: CASEY, IZZY, PEYTON, AND AVERY

Let's meet four personas that represent each of the four Behavioral Styles:

Casey

Casey is a hard-charging thinker who usually sits in the front of the room. Typically well dressed and image-conscious, Casey wants to accomplish big things and can come across as assertive, maybe even pushy, about their ideas. Casey loves to strategize and craves **control**.

Quote that represents Casey: "Strategy is a style of thinking, a conscious and deliberate process." - Pete Johnson

Who do you know that resembles Casey? Write their name here:

_____

Izzy

Izzy is a people person, a facilitator, who gravitates toward connecting with others and ideas. Izzy is typically loaded with possibilities about everything and appears to think quickly on their feet. Izzy lives "in the now," craves action, and seeks to **influence** others.

Quote that represents Izzy: "You have to be fast on your feet and adaptive or else a strategy is useless." - Charles de Gaulle

Who do you know that resembles Izzy? Write their name here:

_____

Peyton

Peyton is a workhorse who is engrossed in work and thrives on to-do lists. Peyton likes sticking to the plan and will **power** through almost anything to achieve desired results. Peyton's goal is to produce large volumes of work and do it quickly!

Quote that represents Peyton: "In reality, strategy is actually very straightforward. You pick a general direction and implement like hell." - Jack Welch

Who do you know that resembles Peyton? Write their name here:

_____

Avery

Avery is an analyzer who loves to focus on gathering information to get into the details. Avery lives in the past and wants to get everything exactly right—all of the time, and so needs to become an **authority** on a particular topic before being able to push forward with a decision.

Quote that represents Avery: "However beautiful the strategy, you should occasionally look at the results." - Sir Winston Churchill

Who do you know that resembles Avery? Write their name here:

_____

Casey, Izzy, Peyton, and Avery represent the four Behavioral Styles:

- Casey is a **Control**

- Izzy is an **Influence**

- Peyton is a **Power**

- Avery is an **Authority**

Now let's examine each of the four Styles in greater detail, beginning with an understanding of how each of the four Styles deals with threats in their environments.

SURVIVAL STRATEGIES IN NATURE

As we have outlined, humans are unique in that we are able to detect (and often struggle to discern between) two types of risk—actual and perceived—while other species experience only actual risk. Since how humans relate to the world complicates things a bit, let's simplify survival behavior by observing how other animals react when facing threatening situations so we can learn about ourselves at a core level.

In nature, we consistently find that animals use one of the four following strategies to preserve their lives. They are summarized in this matrix that examines flight or fight in more detail:

	Fight	Flight
External		
Internal		

Essentially the diagram outlines how some survival strategies are more overt (or External) and other survival strategies that are more covert (or Internal). External means pushing out, while Internal means pushing down.

Let's look at the diagram and go through each one individually:

The first survival strategy easily identifiable in nature is to: **Dictate**.

	Fight	Flight
External	**Dictate**	
Internal		

Some species just have a way of *taking charge of their situation.* When faced with pressure, they tend to take **control** and tackle the threat head-on. Animals such as rhinos, sharks, and lions will attack any animal that tries to move in on their territory. While other animals, such as beavers, are prone to manipulate their environment through actions like cutting down trees, building dams, and re-routing water. These approaches fall under the heading of "Dictate" because, in the face of pressure, these animals take control and force the situation into an outcome that they intend.

The second survival strategy identifiable in nature is to: **Migrate**.

	Fight	Flight
External	Dictate	**Migrate**
Internal		

Some species know that their best chance for survival is to *move away* from pressure so they flee the threats posed by other animals or by the change in seasons, and they're built to outrun, outmaneuver, or out-travel the threat. Some examples of animals that use this strategy are deer, antelope, and, of course, birds. Whales also travel thousands of miles every year, literally following the same paths their ancestors have taken for generations, as they look to **influence** their surroundings and move to safer territory to avoid danger.

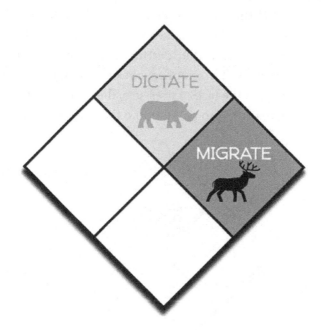

The third survival strategy identifiable in nature is to: **Tolerate**.

	Fight	Flight
	Fight	Flight
External	Dictate	Migrate
Internal	**Tolerate**	

Still other species survive by simply *outworking and outlasting* the threat they face, relying on innate survival characteristics such as protection or disguise. The thick coat of a buffalo insulates it throughout the winter, while a porcupine has tens of thousands of quills that keep predators at bay. Think about a spider—even after you knock down its web multiple times, it keeps building it back in the hopes of catching prey. These types of characteristics allow species like this to **power** through adversity and endure the situation to survive.

The fourth survival strategy identifiable in nature is: **Hibernate**.

	Fight	Flight
	Fight	Flight
External	Dictate	Migrate
Internal	Tolerate	**Hibernate**

A number of animals survive by *pulling back* from their environment, mitigating risk as they do so. Tortoises can safely retract into their shells in the face of a threat. Animals such as bears, rodents, and snakes have the ability to slow their metabolism, allowing them to sleep for extended periods of time during the cold, dark winter months when food is scarce.

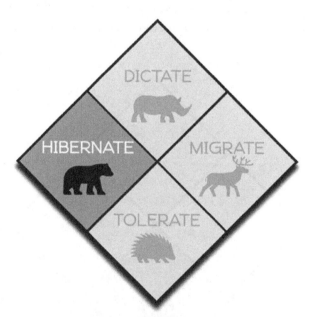

These survival strategies are built into the amygdalae of these species. A rhino's thick hide and powerful horn ensure that it will always charge straight at a problem, while an antelope's fast legs ensure that it will always run away from threats. They do this without thinking—it is wired into them.

Each human has an amygdala too, and so our survival strategy comes pre-loaded into the primitive part of our brains. However, unlike animals, we all pretty much look the same. Without any physical clues then (like shells, horns, or wings), it can be trickier to determine another person's survival strategy, much less our own.

The key is to pay extra-special attention to your own behavior and the behavior of others when we are under pressure. The good news is that there are many clues. When you know what to look and listen for, it will become easier to determine the survival strategies all around you.

SURVIVAL STRATEGIES IN PEOPLE

When humans are under pressure, we are prone to acting very much like reptiles and animals. Once our biology gets triggered, we automatically employ one of these same four survival strategies to manage pressure.

However, unlike other species, we have a highly-evolved neocortex and the ability to use language to explain why we are doing certain things. Using the chart below, let's look at how human beings justify their behavior under pressure, which will further explain the naming architecture of the Styles:

BIOLOGY	NEOCORTEX CONCERN	NEED TO KNOW...	BEHAVIORAL STYLE
DICTATE	Certainty	There is a plan	Control (Casey)
MIGRATE	Freedom	There are options and flexibility	Influence (Izzy)
TOLERATE	Stability	There is a structure	Power (Peyton)
HIBERNATE	Security	How things will ultimately work out	Authority (Avery)

So, if you could hear the internal conversations that each Style has in their head, it would be much easier to know what their Style is.

CONTROL (Casey)

A Control's core concern is for "Certainty." When triggered, the conversation in Casey's head goes something like this: "Whoa, I am not feeling at all certain about how things are going around here, and I don't like it. I don't really understand what's happening, and it doesn't seem like anyone else does either. This situation is totally out of **CONTROL**. So I'm going to dictate and start telling everyone what to do so we can regain that lost sense of certainty. That will make things settle down and start moving in the right direction again."

INFLUENCE (Izzy)

Very different from Control's core concern, an Influence's core concern is for "Freedom." Izzy's pressure-related self-talk sounds like: "I'm feeling really fenced in and restricted right now. My options have been taken away and that makes me feel like I'm being suffocated. I've lost my ability to **INFLUENCE** my environment, and I'm not having any fun anymore. I need freedom again, I need flexibility, and I need to be able to move around. I have to migrate and get the heck out of here!"

"Being slowed down by detail. Right. Like that's the worst thing that can happen to an Influence person."

POWER (Peyton)

A Power's core concern is for "Stability." When Peyton gets triggered, it sounds like: "I don't want to stop making progress. I just want to finish what I started. We can always deal with the problems later, once we've finished what we're working on. Let's just keep things stable and keep working. We just need to **POWER** through this! I hope no one rocks the boat! The best feeling is to check items off my 'to-do' list. Those lists are really important for me so I always know what to do next."

AUTHORITY (Avery)

An Authority's core concern is for "Security." When triggered, the conversation in Avery's head goes something like this: "OK, there's too much information being thrown around without a clear understanding of what it all means. Decisions are starting to be made without considering all the information, which feels really irresponsible. I need to slow things down and think about all this to make sure things turn out OK. I need to protect our future by making sure we make the right decision. So, before I move forward, I need to dig in and become an **AUTHORITY** on the matter."

AN INFLUENCE ADJUSTING TO THE NEEDS OF AUTHORITIES

"I am an Influence and I'm most energized when I'm coming up with new ways of solving my clients' problems. My true nature is to focus on new ideas and new angles—out-of-the-box thinking. But, when I am selling to an Authority person, I spend most of my time on the opposite. Typically, I want to get to an answer quickly, you know, keep things moving. But I've learned that Authorities don't like that at all. It makes them uncomfortable. They want to take time to process things, go over all of the information. Like, all of it! I'll be honest, when I feel we're getting hung up on the details or I feel like the

Continued...

process isn't moving as fast as want, I can feel my biology get triggered. I'm much more aware of that now. So,
instead of following my nature in those moments, I force
myself to remember theirs and I work on slowing things
down, making things more palatable to them so that they
don't struggle with me as much. It's proven to be a useful
strategy for me—I used to struggle, now I just get creative in how I present to them, and I feel like I connect
with them a lot better."

Understanding these core concerns is a great way to observe Styles
in people. The next time you notice someone being triggered by
a situation (especially if you're not feeling the same way), simply
ask yourself if they seem to be concerned by a lack of *Certainty*
(CONTROL), *Freedom (INFLUENCE)*, *Stability (POWER)* or *Security*
(AUTHORITY).

"There are three things extremely hard . . . steel, a diamond, and to know one's self."

— Benjamin Franklin

WHAT IS YOUR BEHAVIORAL STYLE?

The Latin phrase *temet nosce* means "know thyself." Attributed to
Socrates, the ancient Greek aphorism speaks to the importance of

self-awareness. Self-awareness is the quality that most clearly distinguishes humans from all other animals on the planet. It is the ability to hold thoughts about yourself, to simultaneously be an observer of you while you are also being you. It is, no doubt, a tricky proposition.

> *Temet Nosce* is the motto of Hamilton College and Itek University. It was also used by the Wachowski Brothers as the inscription over the Oracle's door in the movie *The Matrix*. Unlike Neo, you will not need to visit a mysterious woman who smokes cigarettes and bakes cookies and has the power of foresight. All you need to do is take a Styles Indicator assessment.

STYLES INDICATOR

Now let's determine *your* style! Are you a Control, Influence, Power, or Authority? Go to http://diamondgoldfish.com to take our Market Force Styles Indicator Assessment.

Note: You'll need to grab the 8-digit code located on page 269 of this book to access your complimentary assessment.

Circle your style: I am a **CONTROL INFLUENCE POWER AUTHORITY**

STYLES PROFILES

Let's take an up-close and personal look at each of the four styles to learn how to identify them, interact with them, and communicate with them:

CONTROL: CASEY THE "DIRECTOR"

People of this Style are often characterized as being independent or strong-willed. They are decisive, and they expect direct answers from those around them. They are determined to make things happen, usually conveying a clear idea of what they want to accomplish before they begin working. They may become critical of others when things don't go their way. Best categorized organizationally as visionaries or entrepreneurs, they are creative and bring astonishing new ideas to the world. They work impressively by themselves, although they can fall into a mode of procrastination without an impending deadline. People of this Style crave immediate results and may have a low tolerance for the feelings of others. They are good at advising self-improvement, but, if not careful, this skill can deteriorate into micro-management and demoralizing criticism. People of this Style often find it difficult to share leadership and can be argumentative when others do not see things their way. They accept challenges and prefer things to be accomplished at a fast pace. When they are at their best, they are magnanimous and generous, using their strength to improve the lives of others. These are thinking people who seek competence in themselves and others. They need to understand life.

Communication style: Direct, "tell it like it is." Focused on the bottom line, they communicate with a purpose, preferring to skip any idle "chitchat." They use verbal skills to mentor others and do not take criticism well. Their talking skills are stronger and more refined than their listening skills.

How to talk to them: Be clear, specific, and brief but do not over-simplify. Present possibilities in a logical fashion with an overview of the relevant facts, and then move to potential solutions. Focus on the anticipated results for the future. Keep the pace fast and decisive, geared toward long-term objectives. Avoid wasting their time with "touchy-feely" conversations or behaviors that could block the path to results. Do not review the past!

INFLUENCE: IZZY THE "CONNECTOR"

People of this Style are often characterized as enthusiastic, talkative, and stimulating. They are empathetic and sensitive, oftentimes putting the needs of others above their own. They usually have a positive attitude toward people and are outgoing, persuasive, and friendly. Most people find them easy to get to know and to be around. They are good at multi-tasking, operate on intuition, and flourish in a flexible environment. They will, however, sometimes cut corners in order to stay ahead of others. People of this Style can be undisciplined with their time and often find it hard to follow through on their commitments. If overextended, they may deteriorate into endless chatter and become a distraction, scattering their energy and leaving many projects unfinished. They do love a good challenge though and are competitive and not deterred by situations. People of this Style are dramatic entertainers, often using exaggeration as a means of effective storytelling. They like getting recognition and are attracted to success and positions of prestige. At their best, they are able to shape the environment and negotiate differences in a way that produces momentum. These are perceptive people who must be free to act. They find joy in being impulsive and acting upon the idea of the moment—"free spirits."

Communication style: They like to talk. They may talk too much or too long and consequently "oversell" or stray off the topic. They talk about ideas and feelings, and many times generalize the facts. They listen for relationship oriented words and may not remember project details. They quickly develop communication openness with others. They communicate for the sake of momentum and use their verbal skills to win people over.

How to talk to them: Plan time to communicate, preferably in a casual environment. Be friendly, ask questions, stay on topic, be open, express feelings, and have fun. Keep the pace fast, spontaneous, and stimulating. Avoid telling them what to do and never assign them boring or repetitive tasks.

POWER: PEYTON THE "BUILDER"

People of this Style are characterized as diligent, agreeable, and dependable. They enjoy implementing structures to create stability and consistency for everyone involved. They thrive on managing many projects at once, feeling as though having lots to do makes life meaningful. People of this Style tend to say "yes" to any and all requests made of them, causing over-involvement and an abundance of stress. They may have difficulty prioritizing their numerous tasks, which can lead to inefficiency in their results. They may express "frustration" when things are not going their way. They work steadily and cohesively with others; always making sure everyone is included in the process. As a result, they have an excellent ability to create alliances and gain support from others. While they dislike personal conflict, if they perceive that their indispensability within a group is threatened, they may begin to gossip or blame others for project failures. People of this style approach risk cautiously and are somewhat resistant to change. Trust and loyalty are very important to them. At their best, they are sympathetic, dependable, and generous, and help to build interpersonal team connections. These are industrious people who produce great amounts of tangible value and seek to be accepted by all.

Communication style: Their speaking is less direct, and it may take them time to develop an open form of communication. They may not speak their feelings openly, choosing instead to show them in action (i.e., by slamming a door). They actively listen to others, and they enjoy using their verbal skills to promote unity and consensus. They avoid confrontation and may even say what others want to hear in order to be accepted.

How to talk to them: Focus on the nuts and the bolts, and demonstrate that they will be included in the process. Present new ideas gently and provide them with guarantees and time to "let the seed grow." Be agreeable and sincere. Concentrate on the specifics of "how" things will get done and draw out their suggestions and opinions. Ask them what is on their list and then don't interrupt until they're done. Keep the pace casual and personal, yet remain focused on the production goals. Avoid pushy, aggressive behavior and don't disrupt their work with conceptual conversations about the future.

AUTHORITY: AVERY THE "PROTECTOR"

People of this Style are typically the rational, orderly type, ultimately concerned with maintaining high quality and standards. They dislike waste and sloppiness. Authority types are often characterized as conscientious, disciplined, and serious. They like things to be logical, organized, and to comply with any preexisting rules. People of this Style are persistent when seeking clarification, often asking very specific questions about the minutest of details. They are deliberate and cautious before taking action, and many times work backward to reach their decisions by using a process of elimination. Most prefer to work by themselves in an objective, task-oriented, intellectual environment. They may be hypersensitive to criticism and can deteriorate into moodiness or counterattacks when they believe others perceive them as incompetent, unprepared, or disorganized. At their best, they are discerning and rigorous, often calling a group back to its root values. These are exacting, judging individuals who thrive on their work. They demand professionalism, organization, and efficiency.

Communication style: They keep their distance communication-wise and rarely ever mingle. Oftentimes they conceal their true feelings and ideas when first asked, preferring instead to think through an entire topic before answering. People of this Style focus on the details and consistently remember them. Typically, they communicate well with the written word. Their ability to listen is stronger than their ability to speak and communicate, though frequently they will use their verbal skills to share their opinions.

How to talk to them: Be prepared and organized. Present details along with the pros and cons. Document everything. Give solid evidence, be serious, and allow time for questions. Do not force a decision. Listen respectfully and take notes regarding their assessments. Keep the pace systematic and formal. Avoid surprises, inconsistency, and unpredictability.

USING THE MAPPING SYSTEM

Now that you know your Behavioral Style, let's review the Styles framework. With the understanding of business as a game and with the awareness of different survival strategies in nature, let's look at the different distinctions among the four Behavioral Styles.

These distinctions are intended to encourage you to realize that *we are not all watching the same movie.* Even when we all find ourselves in the exact same situation, based on our individual Styles, we will tend to experience moments very differently from one another.

To make it easier for you to visualize, we want to introduce you to our simple mapping system. The basic map looks like a large "plus sign" with the Control Style at the top, Influence on the right, Power at the bottom, and Authority on the left.

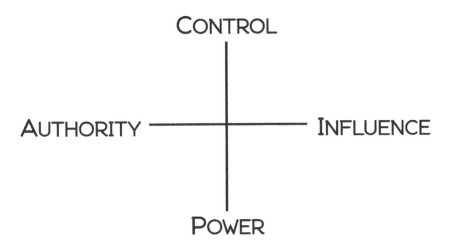

Every distinction will be presented in this format, and each distinction will give you a flavor of what it is like to experience the world through the eyes of each of the Styles. If you would, take a quick moment to draw the map on a piece of paper, with a C, I, P, and A around the plus sign in the middle. The more you do this, the more you create an anchor for the Styles system.

Before we jump in, let's talk about your mindset. We want you to think of the map as a topographical map, which is a 2-dimensional method for representing a 3-dimensional world. Every time you use or draw one of the maps, think about how you are overlaying maps on top of each other to help you view things from a slightly different perspective. Styles distinctions do not exist independently from each other; when you see the distinctions as overlaying on themselves, it will create a greater depth of understanding.

There are two primary benefits to using this Style mapping technology:

1. It creates a common language. When a group of people uses the Styles map, they share a common language, thereby allowing them to quickly relate to a new situation in the same way. This approach facilitates learning and allows you and your team to act quickly.

2. It simplifies the game. Human dynamics in business can be difficult. Visuals tend to make things easier to understand. As you work with our mapping system, you may find it is much more effective to explain challenging situations to others by drawing the plus sign surrounded by the four letters of C, I, P, and A.

HAVING A MAP IS REALLY HELPFUL

"Yeah, the maps are killer. I think they work really well regardless of what your Style is. They help you get really clear about your own biology quickly, which is a great reminder that your survival needs can get in the way of your sales efforts. Once I'm able to get my biology under control, then I'm able to focus on what the other person needs. The maps show me what's most important to them, which allows me build and grow my relationships with others. It's amazing. It's brilliant because it's simple."

To assist you in your discovery, over the next four chapters we'll walk you through 10 Styles distinctions:

- 3 Survival Characteristics

- 4 Desires

- 2 50/50s

- 1 Key for Building Trust

We'll start at the top of the Styles distinctions list with the three survival characteristics.

CHAPTER 5

SURVIVAL CHARACTERISTICS

"I was taught that the human brain was the crowning glory of evolution so far, but I think it's a very poor scheme for survival."

— Kurt Vonnegut

Each Style has a distinct approach it uses to survive and protect itself from real risk. In a real risk environment, this approach would be the best chance for each Style to live. However, the game of business is not a real risk game, so engaging your Survival Strategy in business situations usually results in damage to your reputation. Let's look at survival strategies, survival concerns, and greatest fears for each of the four behavioral styles:

1. Survival Strategies

Once their Survival Strategy has been identified, people can choose whether to engage their biological response or move to another more appropriate strategy, creating more flexibility in the environment of how we all handle pressure.

FLEXIBILITY IS KEY TO MAKING THE DIAMOND RULE WORK

"I've learned that what's most important in terms of the Diamond Rule is the ability to flex to make sure that others are getting what they need from me. This is different based on what their Style is, from the way that they like to work, how they like to receive information, how they like to buy. When I allow their needs to drive my interactions with them — rather than what I think they should be doing — I find that I can zero in on what reduces pressure for them, and that makes all the difference! In the past I would say things like, 'Well, that's not really my management style' or 'I don't work that way' or 'that client really shouldn't be responding to our proposal like that'. But, now I see how that always led me down the

Continued...

wrong road, further away from solving their problems. When you have that mindset, you're going away from productivity because one of the greatest things you learn from the Diamond Rule is that your own Style is not the most important thing. The most important thing is your understanding of how other people operate. Since I developed the ability to flex so others get what they need in order to move things forward not only am I able to get a higher performance out of my team, I am consistently able to generate more sales more quickly because I make things easier for others."

Let's look at how each of the four behavioral Styles employ their Survival Strategy:

CONTROLS

A Control's natural Survival Strategy is to want to **DICTATE** under pressure. People of this Style tend to relate to a bigger-picture perspective, and they want to have certainty of direction for where a project is going over the course of time. Without that certainty, Controls will often complain that a team "has no clear strategy," or that they "don't understand where things are going." When they begin to feel this way, a Control's natural response is to dictate and simply start telling people what to do in order to calm their biology. This can lead Controls to be seen as "pushy" or "demanding" by others.

INFLUENCES

An Influence's natural Survival Strategy is to want to **MIGRATE** under pressure. People of this Style tend to live in the moment, and when things around them start to feel constrained, Influences may feel as though their freedom is being compromised. When this happens, Influences may complain that they feel "fenced in" or "restricted," and their tendency is to look for options and "outs" in order to calm their biology. They may tend to go one direction one day, then another the next day, which can be useful in a chaotic time, but it can be destabilizing if the team needs structure. Such a natural approach can lead Influences to be seen as "flighty," "scattered," or "all over the place" by others.

AN INFLUENCE OWNING THE ANIMAL NATURE OF THEIR STYLE

"I remember the very first time I was introduced to the Diamond Rule. In that training they made the point that human behavior under pressure is a lot like these different animals they showed us. My first thought was, 'Are these guys being serious? What, we're going to be like 'this person's a lion' and 'that person's a snake', like these, you know, spirit animals?' At first I thought it was pretty far out there, but when they explained how different animals survive in the wild, using examples of a rhinoceros, birds, buffalo, and a tortoise, and related them to how humans act when they find themselves under pressure, I really got it. It turned out to be fascinating to me because my favorite animal has always been a hawk. Being an Influence myself and realizing a bird is what I already identify with, it just struck me as like, 'Oh, okay, there might be something to all of this!' From this first connection to the material I have stayed open-minded and tried to observe what my biology wants to do when the pressure ticks up, and for me, it's often to take flight."

POWERS

A Power's natural Survival Strategy is to want to **TOLERATE** under pressure. People of this Style tend to live in the short term (say 90 days into the future) and are more focused on producing tangible results more than the other Styles. This perspective can lead them to complain that "we are changing things too often" or "we are looking too far down the road." When these complaints start, Powers tend to want more stability to calm their biology. Powers then tend to grind through more work and will persevere—all of which is good until they take on too much work and become the ultimate tolerator, or, in other words, a "pushover." When that happens, Powers often become the scapegoat for the entire team's or organization's failure to get things done.

AUTHORITIES

An Authority's natural Survival Strategy is to want to **HIBER-NATE** under pressure. People of this Style tend to focus primarily on the past and like to review trends to figure out what to do next. When things are "moving too fast," Authorities will instinctively want to slow things down to calm their biology. They want to ensure the right decisions are being made. This makes Authorities feel more secure. If timed appropriately, this helps keep a project on track. Done too often, others will begin to feel that the Authority is a "roadblock" to progress, and the other Styles may begin to avoid them for fear of things slowing down too much.

A CONTROL AND AN AUTHORITY OVERCOMING THEIR BIOLOGIES TO PROVIDE GREATER CLIENT VALUE

"There's an Authority I work with on my sales team who used to drive me crazy. He'd always insert himself into

Continued...

deals at the wrong time and just take all the wind out of my sail. He'd throw up roadblocks and make things harder than they had to be. It felt like we were working against each other, even though we were on the same team. As a Control, I love coming up with out-of-the-box ideas to help my prospects see ways through their current challenges, but my Authority colleague would always point out why those ideas won't work, and we'd just look stupid in front of the client.

"I couldn't take it any longer. We had to figure this out. So, I had a heart-to-heart with him about this problem. It actually turned out to be a great conversation. We were both able to express our frustrations with each other, and when I saw how much our Market Force Styles were at play, it actually became a little comical. I was coming from my biology just as much as he was, and we were in that classic Control-Authority breakdown where I would create something new in the future because it solved a problem I was having today and he would seek to validate the concept based on evidence from the past. I mean it was exactly like it was explained in the training.

"Once we recommitted to being on the same team, we coordinated our contributions, so we came across as completely aligned to our clients. We agreed that I would listen for opportunities to creatively solve client problems and then I would express them with the caveat that my Authority partner would do the research to determine the feasibility of the concept. In this way, we were both able to contribute from our areas of strength but coordinate our contributions in such a way that we came across as a

Continued...

team. We actually started delivering even better ideas as a result of his involvement and started to consistently win more deals. All we had to do was overcome our biologies and commit to something bigger than ourselves."

2. Survival Concerns

Human beings invented language, and one of the usages of language is to describe why we do what we do under pressure. This means that each Style's Survival Strategy is interpreted in language as a Survival Concern, the primary thing that upsets each of us and throws us into our habitual response to pressure. Once we have awareness of our Survival Concern, we can again choose to allow it to inform our next moves or we can choose to focus on something else, knowing we won't die in the game of business.

CONTROLS

A Control's Survival Concern is for **CERTAINTY**. Certainty is not a concern for the final outcome (which we would define as security); instead, it is a concern for understanding the direction where things are headed. Controls are naturally focused on a five-year time frame and ideas and visions for where things should go in the future. In the absence of having their certainty of direction, Controls may drop into a default mode and begin dictating to others what they should do. This can lead others to perceive them as arrogant. Positioned appropriately, their perspective can help others feel that there is a long-term strategy in place.

INFLUENCES

An Influence's Survival Concern is for **FREEDOM**. Influences like to work in chaos, often creating chaos if there is none because it allows them to feel completely unrestrained. Their moment-to-moment time frame and natural focus on relationships means that Influences are often easy to be around in a non-work environment as they are very personable and spontaneous. But this behavior can be difficult for the other Styles to partner with on a daily basis. This commitment to freedom may lead Influences to move from project to project or even job to job as a migration strategy in the game of business. Positioned appropriately, their perspective can help a team get a number of projects started as Influences tend to be naturally good at engaging and influencing others to move forward.

AN INFLUENCE SELLING TO THE NEEDS OF A CONTROL

"As an Influence person I'm very concerned about my relationships with others. If somebody doesn't like me, boy my biology kicks in, like immediately. I can feel it in my chest, and it almost feels like I'm going to die. So, of course, I do everything I can to prevent that from happening, which often looks like some kind of theatrics to get them to like me. One of the things that learning the Market Force methodology made me realize is that my need to be liked has really hurt my chances of selling to the Control Style. I've learned that Control people really need a lot of certainty, they focus on ideas and strategy, and they need to know that you know what you're doing to make them feel comfortable. So when I would focus on 'Oh I'm going to create

Continued...

such a great relationship with this person,' that was actually the last thing on their mind. They have ideas of what they want to accomplish, and they just want to know how my company is going to help them solve those problems. So, it's a struggle for me as an Influence, but I have to contain my own needs, and when I can get them excited about our capabilities, I make that mean that they like me!"

POWERS

A Power's Survival Concern is for **STABILITY**. Powers tend to be more pragmatic than the other Styles, focusing more on the structure for how we are going to get things done than where exactly we are going. Their 90-day time frame leads them to desire results, and things that interfere in their process tend to make them feel as though things are unstable. This commitment to stability may lead Powers to take on too much work in order to feel busy (therefore stable), leading other Styles to overload them unintentionally. Positioned appropriately, their perspective can help a team get a number of projects completed as Powers tend to be naturally good at "getting stuff done."

A POWER ADJUSTING TO THE NEEDS OF AN INFLUENCE PROSPECT

"As a Power I am really good in the sales process at delivering on what my prospects need to help move the deal forward. We work pretty big deals that have a long

Continued...

sales cycle, so we need to continuously show value along the way. For whatever reason, most of the prospects I've worked with are Controls who tend to be very direct and give clear direction on what they need, and then I do what I do, which is complete the tasks quickly to keep the process moving.

"Then one day, a new opportunity came along with an Influence prospect, and I had never really worked with an Influence before and hadn't fully appreciated the difference between these two Styles. But it became very apparent to me. It seems with an Influence that they have a new thought about what they want from me about every 10 minutes or so! I found myself struggling because I'd leave a meeting with 10 things to do. Then, when I would catch back up a week later and report on those items, the prospect would say to me, 'When did I ask for these?' or 'Why did you work on this?' I was getting so frustrated!

"Then I remembered my Market Force training and realized that I was dealing with an entirely different animal. I changed my approach and started to make sure that a request was actually a request, rather than just a spur of the moment thing to focus on. I completely shifted to only complete tasks he asked for to about 15% (as opposed to 85% for my Control prospects) and then check in to make sure this was still something he wanted. This was a big shift for me in terms of appreciating the person on the other side of the table and understanding how different perspectives can be. These changes made a big difference because I was now able really focus my efforts where they could make the biggest difference."

AUTHORITIES

An Authority's Survival Concern is for **SECURITY**. Authorities tend to want the details and to make sure they understand everything from every angle. Their time frame of the past and analytical approach tends to lead them to focus on efficiency over speed and quality over quantity every time. Their commitment to the security of the outcome may lead the other Styles to see them as "risk-averse" and avoid them anytime a new project starts. Positioned appropriately, their perspective can help a team avoid needless problems by seeing where there are issues before the delivery of a project to customers.

A POWER ADJUSTING TO THE NEEDS OF AUTHORITY CLIENTS

"Many of my clients are Authorities, and I have been challenged to work successfully with them for most of my career, which as a Power is a big deal, because working well with others is practically our calling card.

"Learning and appreciating that Authorities are going to struggle with decision-making has been really powerful for me. I use that awareness to shift into the Diamond Rule and look for ways to treat Authorities the way they want to be treated, prioritizing security, making sure that I've completed all the analysis on everything before pushing forward to completion, versus the way I like to work, which is making checklists and powering through things quickly.

"I recently had a situation with an Authority client who was having an issue with a report I provided to him.

Continued...

He was unsettled about some of the changes in the report, and he wanted to talk through them. So I thought, 'OK, I know he is going to have lots of questions. He's going to want to vet all the facts and want extra information but is ultimately still going to struggle to make a decision.' Knowing this, I walked through all of the analysis, sharing all of the in-depth thought we put into making this change to the report. We also talked about why we felt so good about this change. And then at the end, I just stated very frankly for him, 'I recommend this change. We've really thought this one through. But that's only if you agree.' By stating my opinion in that moment, rather than leaving the decision solely to him, I think I helped relieve some pressure.

"He was able to just quickly agree and say, 'Yes, we've been through all the facts; you've been through all the data. Let's make this change and move forward.' And at the end of that conversation, he actually said, 'You know, when I got on this call, I was really just very worked up about having to think about making this change, wondering if were we going to make this change or if we were not going to make this change, and you just really calmed me down.' I thought, 'That is the Market Force material at work!' I knew exactly what I was doing the whole time. I knew I was calming him down. It was one of those moments where you go, 'This really works. The Diamond Rule really does work.' "

3. Greatest Fears

Fear is an essential element of survival. Fear is what alerts your amygdala to the presence of a threat, which in turn, triggers you into action to save yourself. And, while all Styles will get similarly triggered in the case of real risk—like stepping in front of a moving vehicle or facing a growling dog—in the case of perceived risk, things vary wildly based on your Style.

Each Style has its own version of a *Greatest Fear*—the type of pressure scenario that most easily triggers you into believing that your life is actually at stake. The major concern is that if you don't have a handle on your *Greatest Fear*, it has a way of taking over your life, causing things to be much harder than they need to be. Remember, when you play the game of business as if there is a life-or-death risk, you will likely act in ways that are detrimental to achieving your intended future.

USING STYLES TO BUILD PROPOSALS THAT APPEAL TO ALL

"After I learned about Styles, I put a much greater focus on making sure that my sales proposals always include important pieces for all four Styles. I used to only put my attention on what my prospect said they needed, but I've had that backfire on me several times when a different decision-maker would get involved last minute and not see what was important to them. I realized that you never really know who will be looking at the proposal, so now I do my best to appeal to all the Styles every time. For example, I always lead with a high-level, executive

Continued...

summary because Controls just want to understand the big picture. Powers want to know that there's some realistic structure in there about how we intend to deliver on what we're promising. Authorities seem to go to straight to the bottom line to get that security, and they really will read everything you give them, so I try to give them a lot! Finally, Influences really want to focus on the relationship, so they're not that interested in what's in the proposal, just that I'm making them look good. This approach has really improved our hit rate as everyone gets what they need."

CONTROLS

A Control's *Greatest Fear* is: "If others know that I don't know something *I should know*, then I will die." Since Controls want to be seen as the ones everyone goes to for answers, they need to position themselves as *already knowing everything that's going on.* So, their *Greatest Fear* is not being omniscient. You can hear this in their automatic responses when you are telling them something, "Yep, uh-huh, I know." Controls tend to hold firm to their positions when faced with conflicting viewpoints unless you are very good at providing convincing evidence. But if your approach instead is to try to prove them wrong, you will likely find that Controls become more interested in being right than having things work, and that approach will get you nowhere. If a Control cannot see the efficacy of other people's contributions, they will automatically characterize them as idiots and remove themselves from conversations to work in isolation in search of a grand solution to a problem so that they can once again be seen as "all-knowing."

INFLUENCES

An Influence's *Greatest Fear* is: "If I have to do what other people tell me to do, then I will die." This is true even when they 100 percent agree with what they are being told to do. It just comes down to choice, and when they feel they don't have any, it is crippling to them. Influences have a strong commitment to the feeling of freedom and will avoid participating in situations where their freedom may be compromised. In other words, they will not be a member of any club that requires them to be or do something. Seeking different possibilities that have few restrictions and little established criteria, they are in constant search for the "ultimate rush" even if what's required is a bit of structure and follow-through. Influences treasure flexibility and challenges. Routine tasks tend not to be their strength.

POWERS

The *Greatest Fear* a Power has is: "If I am not included, I will die." Powers are loyal team members, almost to a fault. Their need to be included can cause Powers to say "yes" to every ask made of their time. The end result is that they are often over-extended and many Powers actually experience "burnout" earlier than other Styles in their careers simply due to overworking themselves. If they are in a role that can have a lot of rejection, such as cold calling, oftentimes they will struggle more than the other Styles due to this Survival Conversation.

AUTHORITIES

An Authority's *Greatest Fear* is: "If I have to choose without all of the information under the sun, I will die." Authorities like to keep their options open by not killing alternatives. They tend to avoid movement in any one direction in the hope of preserving the status quo in a way that will make their lives less chaotic and more predictable. This inability to make a decision without assurance of the outcome may cause Authorities to spend exorbitant amounts of time in "what if" scenarios. This will have them evade action until there are no options left or they just get left behind when others decide it is time to move on.

SUMMARIZING SURVIVAL ATTRIBUTES

Here is a thumbnail for how each behavior handles threats to their survival:

CONTROLS

A Control has a Survival Strategy to **DICTATE** under pressure, driven by their innate concern for understanding where things are going in the future. In the absence of that certainty of direction, Controls can become quite demanding of others with questions like "What did you not understand about my idea?" This approach to pressure tends to come from the need to already know everything in advance and can lead to Controls being seen by others as "difficult to work with."

A POWER SALES TEAM LEADER WORKING EFFECTIVELY WITH A CONTROL SALESPERSON

"I'm a Power and I have a salesperson on my team who is a Control. I've learned that maybe this isn't the best reporting structure for her. I can tell she gets uncomfortable sometimes about whether or not I am leading us in the right direction, whether or not she is getting the training she needs to be successful, and whether or not I am providing her with enough context for the things I

Continued...

need her to get done. I know those things are important to her, but sometimes I forget to present things in a way that satisfies her need for certainty.

"I end up spending a lot of time talking her down off the ledge because she needs to be reassured that even though she doesn't feel completely in control that together we can make sure we are controlling the situation. I work up plans to show her she is going to get all the resources that she needs.

"In the past, I would have taken all of this personally and gotten offended that she doesn't trust my leadership. But the Diamond Rule has allowed me to remember that for a Control, my leadership role is to create certainty so that she can have a comfort level about where we are going, why, and how that will help her be successful. Once that happens, it's a big relief to her, and she's like, 'OK. I'm good.' And then we are able to cruise on and continue working productively for our clients."

INFLUENCES

An Influence has a Survival Strategy to **MIGRATE** under pressure, driven by their innate concern for freedom and flexibility. Once an Influence begins to feel as though there is too much structure or too much process, they can become quite impatient to leave the environment in order to reduce their anxiety. This approach to pressure tends to come from the concern for avoiding domination by others at all costs and can lead to Influences being seen by others as "a nice person, but unreliable."

POWERS

A Power has a Survival Strategy to **TOLERATE** under pressure, driven by their innate concern for being an indispensable part of the team. When Powers start to feel as though they are not busy enough, they view it as instability in the environment. Their approach may be to take on more work to try to prove that they should have "a seat at the table" for every project. This approach to tolerating pressure tends to lead Powers to become overextended and even to be seen by others as the "pushover" on the team.

AUTHORITIES

An Authority has a Survival Strategy to **HIBERNATE** under pressure, driven by their innate concern to avoid making a bad decision that could lead to a bad result. When Authorities begin to feel as though their security is threatened by a wrong choice, they begin looking for any reason to avoid making a commitment. This approach to pressure tends to lead Authorities to want to move slower than the other Styles, which can frustrate those around them so much that they actually begin to avoid inviting Authorities to meetings because "we never make a decision when he/she is in the room."

AN AUTHORITY ACCEPTING HIS TRUE NATURE

"For me, knowing who I really am at my core, and that I don't have to be something that I am not, is quite encouraging. There are Authorities out in the world that I respect and know, and it's okay to be who we are—people

Continued...

who look to increase the standards and the quality of everything we touch. I mean I don't think I could change it any more than I could change the color of my eyes or the color of my hair. But knowing that it's okay for my body to react the way it does in breakdowns or those visceral moments, it's okay. There's nothing wrong with me. It's just the way I'm made and that's fine, even if I'm different than people around me. That is very reassuring and gives me the foundation from which I can work my way out of the pressure."

As promised, we'll now move on to the second item on our list of Styles distinctions and examine what each Style desires.

CHAPTER 6

DESIRED IDENTITY

"If your survival strategy runs your sales game, it will compromise your reputation."

— Travis Carson

In this chapter, we highlight areas that people tend to most naturally focus on and desire as a result of their Style. Since we all tend to get good at the things we do the most, these are typically the areas where each Style develops their greatest skill. In other words, these tend to be the areas of the greatest individual assets, strengths, and advantages. But, to be clear, we are by no means limiting what each Style can or cannot do. Instead, we are illustrating the natural tendencies associated with each Style, based on their natural wiring.

Together we'll take a look at the desired identity, time frame, learning preference, and pace for each of the four behavioral Styles.

EACH STYLE'S DESIRED IDENTITY

As we explained earlier in the book, business is a game played for identity. In other words, it's all about your reputation with the people you work with. Each Style is most naturally wired for one of four business positions, even if that business position is not in their job title.

CONTROLS

The most natural business position for a Control is in the area of **MARKETING**. Marketing is the practice of developing convincing arguments and approaches to support the adoption of new ideas. This is how Controls naturally tend to think. Controls focus on the identity part of the game, so branding fits right into that area. Whether they are on a sales team with clients in the external market or they work for the accounting department within a large firm, Controls enjoy the process of finding and simplifying new ideas that could satisfy needs. They are future-oriented people, creational, and thought-oriented. Controls are wired for helping to build identity.

INFLUENCES

The most natural business position for an Influence is in **SALES**. Influences love to make connections with people and with ideas. Sales is the process of building relationships to bring forth new possibilities, which is something that comes naturally to Influences. Again, even if we are talking about an accounting team, if there is an Influence on the team, he or she is most likely the one reaching out to users of the data to make sure they are getting what they need (i.e., doing sales for the accounting team!). Influences are focused on other people's concerns over their own, are action-oriented, and crave freedom. All of which aligns well for someone in a sales role.

POWERS

A Power's most natural business position is in **PRODUCTION**. Production is the process of establishing an effective structure for following through on all of the promises we have made to our clients (whether those clients are internal or external). Powers naturally focus on tangible results and what we "have to do," making them perfect to oversee the operations for any high performing team. They are also strong at building team unity and furthering growth objectives by including everyone in the process. Powers are naturally focused on the next 90 days, are action-oriented, and preservational. These are all perfect traits for heading up production.

AUTHORITIES

An Authority's most natural business position is in **ADMINIS-TRATION**. Administration is the evaluation and reflection on past performance in order to distinguish effective from ineffective action. Given that Authorities most naturally focus on the past, they are very strong at making sure the quality and the execution is satisfactory to deliver to clients (whether those clients are internal or external). Detail-oriented, thought-oriented, and preservational by nature, Authorities can provide a team with tremendous security.

With an Authority on board, the other Styles know that nothing will fall through the cracks.

EACH STYLE'S DESIRED TIME FRAME

Each Style has a distinct time frame in which they automatically approach performance and the game of business. In order to orchestrate a project that keeps a positive tempo, it is essential to acknowledge this "timing" element. Once identified for you and others around you, you will be able to more gracefully contribute when it is most appropriate, and then step aside so others can effectively participate.

CONTROLS

A Control has a time frame of **3 TO 5 YEARS** into the future. Their ability to abandon the daily emergencies for the distant future allows them to create new opportunities while others are working toward completing previous commitments. Controls are not particularly adept at deciding what actions need to be taken in the moment to arrive at their envisioned future. So instead of handing off to someone else, Controls may sit on an idea until it is "perfect." By that time, the window of opportunity may be gone. But with their natural time frame added to the process, a team tends to have a better connection with its future strategy.

INFLUENCES

An Influence has a time frame of **MOMENT TO MOMENT**. They have the ability to dance in chaos and execute what can look to the other Styles as an impossible mission without missing a beat. With a heightened sense of presence in uncertain times, Influences are well equipped to listen for the next appropriate move based on current circumstances. Their timing will be off, however, if they are placed in a structured position that restricts freedom of movement and requires repetitious work. In these times, the project may actually "misfire" since Influences tend to be drawn to create chaos when there is none. As a strong team member, Influences will help the team navigate difficult situations in the moment they arise.

AN INFLUENCE'S EXPLANATION OF THEIR COMFORT ZONE

"As an Influence, I've come to realize that I feel most comfortable when I'm operating in the present moment. I strive to bring people together, which you can only do in real time. I really like to connect with others, really get what's going on for them, what's important to them, what drives them, what makes them tick. You know, I think that's what an Influence does. And I try to make everything OK and take care of everybody. That doesn't always work. I've learned that our greatest strength can also be our greatest weakness. I have to fight against that tendency to fix things for other people when they have an issue in the moment, be patient and give them a chance to work things out on their own. I can have challenges with Powers with their focus on the next quarter and for sure with Authorities who focus on the past—sometimes we still butt heads, but I think I get through those issues quicker with the awareness of my biology."

POWERS

A Power has a time frame of **90 DAYS** into the future. This quarterly equivalent is the typical time limit Powers have for their endless "to do" lists in order to ensure completion of their numerous projects. Powers are often seen as running the engine room that makes a team go. As long as the specifics are outlined, Powers are ready. It is when a Power is placed in a position of prioritizing that they can lose their balance. Powers often end up working late at night, under a pile of countless requests and assignments, with more commitments to more projects than they can possibly handle. At that point, Powers move to "management by crisis." Powers are important though, as they are the ones making sure we are getting everything done in order to satisfy our outstanding commitments.

KEEPING A POWER ON HIS TEAM HAPPY AND PRODUCTIVE

"I have a Power on my team, and she's my best producer by a mile. I trust her completely, and she's got this amazing work ethic. Through Market Force, I've learned how to keep her operating in her happy place. I found that when she has a ton of work on her desk, she's much happier. And every time she gets slow, she gets a little grumpy. When she's busy, she feels indispensable to the team and to her clients. In fact, the busier she gets, the more excited and engaged she becomes in her work. I see firsthand how the Diamond Rule helps us both get what we want!"

AUTHORITIES

An Authority has a time frame of the **PAST**. Their natural contribution is the evaluation of previous performances in order to help a team improve in the future. When an Authority is committed to getting rid of everything extraneous to successful project implementation, they are an enormous contributor because the other Styles do not analyze evidence as thoroughly. However, it can be a sign of imminent project delay when an Authority moves out of the past to decide what they think is the best course of action for the future. A strong Authority helps the team stay grounded by consistently learning from the previous outcomes along the way.

AN AUTHORITY OVERCOMING HIS BIOLOGICAL TENDENCY TO FREEZE

"The "aha" moment for me came when I understood who I am at my core. Simply stated, I am an Authority who classically freezes under pressure. I go into hibernation mode, considering all my options, and don't move until I've absolutely thought through every angle of the situation. But I know that doesn't really help me solve problems. It just gets me stuck and sitting on the sidelines. So, what I've learned to do with the awareness of my Style is to push myself into action in those moments, convincing myself it's time to start eating the elephant one bite at a time. I started to trust that I would figure out how to tackle the problem better by doing something rather than just thinking about it. I just have to keep moving forward. It's even to the point where I've told my team to push me. I've told them that if they catch me in a moment of 'uh-oh, now what do I do?' to push me to run right into the problem and get going, because generally when I start moving, the solution sort of shows up. Not how I'm naturally wired, but I've learned to overcome that."

How Each Style Desires to Take In New Information and Learn

When it comes to learning, there is no right or wrong way to do it although each Style appears to have a primary way they default to for taking in new information. This does not mean that each Style can't or won't learn in other ways. But as often as we can as a team, we should be attempting to give each Style what they need biologically in order to maximize growth and accomplishment.

CONTROLS

A Control has a primary learning style of **THINKING**. Controls are always looking for the next best option to accomplish their long-term objective and often "make their money outside of time" by thinking up a new idea, approach, or strategy. Many times their work areas are sparsely furnished to avoid clutter, maybe with a whiteboard for writing down new ideas, and they will often stare out a window while they think of possibilities for how to grow the business. The downside is that many times Controls will expect the other Styles to read their minds and will forget that no one can hear those ideas that they have been thinking about for weeks.

INFLUENCES

An Influence has a primary learning style of **TALKING**. Influences tend to be possibility-oriented, and they get energized when brainstorming with others. They often like to "think out loud" by discussing new ideas and new approaches. Because their natural time frame is "right now," often Influences can move from one idea to another in one conversation after another, which can be difficult on other Styles, especially Powers and Authorities, who are often trying to figure out what they are going to work on once a collaboration with an Influence is over. Conversely, Influences are typically the most flexible of the Styles and can move in and out of new ideas very quickly due to their reliance on conversations for their learning.

POWERS

A Power has a primary learning style of **DOING**. Powers tend to see things in more black and white terms than other Styles. Until they have done something, they won't speculate on how to do it. Powers focus more often on the next 90 days in terms of their natural time frame onto the world, and in order to things to get done in the next quarter, they have to demonstrate that they can execute on it. This perspective can lead to Powers overcommitting themselves to all of the things they think they can do, sometimes underestimating how much work there is to do.

AUTHORITIES

An Authority has a primary learning style of **READING**. Authorities are often the most analytical of all of the Styles, and they tend to enjoy reading through material more than the other Styles. Due to their natural time frame of the past, many times an Authority will ask for something "in writing" so that they have a chance to review and reflect on it before making a decision. When they forget that the other Styles don't like to read as much as they do, Authorities will write long correspondence that will drive the other Styles crazy.

How Each Style Desires Pace

When it comes to working together, different Styles have unique interpretations for how fast or slow we should be moving together, and how much planning or action we should be taking along the way. Again, there is no right or wrong approach; but through awareness, hopefully, the Styles can meet each other in the middle and optimize the outcome of the projects they are working on.

CONTROLS

A Control has a more natural **FAST AND DEMANDING** pace. Controls consistently look for ways to push things in the direction of their vision and can be unrelenting in their desire to see that direction come to life. The downside can be that others can interpret Controls as off-putting and over the top with their pushiness. Sometimes they are even seen as arrogant. However, the upside is that Controls often help those around them exceed their own expectations and potential and achieve more than others ever thought possible.

A CONTROL LEARNING TO TAKE A FRIENDLIER APPROACH TO SOLVING PROBLEMS

"I'm a Control and one of the biggest impacts this aware-ness has had on me is realizing that when my biology kicks, I revert to leading with force. When I don't get my way, I just become more and more forceful. If I couldn't figure out how to solve a problem, I just beat it with a ham-mer. And if that didn't work, I'd just get a bigger hammer! Clearly this approach would work against me in a sales situation! The lesson I've learned is to recognize that this automatic reaction is biology at work and to not be so respectful of it. What I mean by "respectful" is that I have found my biology to feel so right that I assume it must be correct. What Market Force has taught me above all else is to be less respectful of that biology when there is pressure in the air and not to follow it blindly just because it feels so good to beat things with a hammer or whatever your particular Style is. That has made a huge difference for me. It has allowed me to build more respectful and productive relationships with others. I still have the biology, of course, there's that physiological reaction that never goes away. I just recognize it a lot quicker and a lot more often now. I've learned how to let others know how important something is to me without being overly forceful along the way. See how easy that was? No hammers involved."

INFLUENCES

An Influence has a natural **QUICK AND FLEXIBLE** pace. Because Influences tend to be possibility-oriented, they often iterate very quickly and make changes to things in ways that can feel scattered to the other Styles. In many cases, this approach can lead the other Styles to tire of all the changes and feel like things are too chaotic. However, the upside is that Influences typically find new ways of thinking or doing things that can lead to huge breakthroughs for a high-performance team with their "outside the box" way of doing things.

POWERS

A Power has a natural **DILIGENT AND PRAGMATIC** pace. Powers, with their production focus, tend to want to get things into a structure for collaboration and to get things done. Sometimes this approach has a Power stray from having a more strategic conversation around why we are doing certain things (i.e., "We have to get this done, don't ask why!"), which can lead a team to work on unnecessary items. However, to the upside, oftentimes it is a Power on a team bringing everyone back to level ground. This allows the team to have necessary conversations around who is going to do what and by when.

AUTHORITIES

An Authority has a natural **DELIBERATE AND DETAILED** pace. Authorities tend to like to think things through more than any of the other Styles. They have a natural desire for more information, leading them to want extra time to reflect before "just jumping to conclusions." Sometimes the other Styles feel as though an Authority has analysis paralysis. However, the upside of an Authority's approach is that a team will make fewer mistakes and will have their processes better pressure-tested through the perspective of an Authority person on the team.

Now that we've looked at the four desires, let's move to the next item on our list of the Styles distinctions and dive into the two 50/50s.

CHAPTER 7

50/50S

"You can have anything in life you want,
if you just help other people get what they want."

— Zig Ziglar

The aim of this section is to identify certain characteristics of the Styles that are "either/or" distinctions. This approach greatly simplifies your determination of another person's Style, as you only consider one of two characteristics at a time, as opposed to one in four. There are two groups of two that have similar characteristics. We call these 50/50s. The first of the two distinctions is about energy, and the second is about progress.

POSITIONS ON THE FIELD

The first 50/50 category is called "Positions on the Field." It distinguishes *which energy within a project* you are most likely drawn toward, as predicted by your Style. In sports, to win a game, you and your team need to play *both* strong offense and strong defense. The offense would be responsible for scoring the points, putting pressure on the opponent, and creating opportunities. The defense would be responsible for protecting our end of the field and preserving the lead. All good teams know that both positions on the team are necessary and important. And, if they ensure they have the right people in the right roles, those teams increase their overall chances for success.

The 50/50 for Positions on the Field goes like this:

Controls and Influences tend to be more **OFFENSIVE** players, meaning they are naturally inclined to get more things started than finished, whether that is a new project, relationship, or client engagement. Their excitement about these opportunities peaks at the beginning while the opportunities are still being formulated and then tends to wane over time as things become more predictable. Once their interest in the opportunity decreases, they can easily be drawn into something else that feels way more "new," abandoning previous efforts—even when there is still work to do.

On the other side of the team, Powers and Authorities are more **DEFENSIVE** players, meaning they are more inclined to protect the ground already gained than to set out on something new. These Styles typically won't start something unless they are committed to following it through to completion. Powers and Authorities also tend to bring more endurance and task orientation to projects. In contrast to the offensive Styles, Powers and Authorities tend to gain interest in projects as they move forward, getting energized by digging into tangible activities and outcomes.

In summary, Controls and Influences tend to be the more creational players while Powers and Authorities play more of a preservational role.

When we remember that successful teams—championship teams— need both types of players, we can learn to engage in those activities that will most benefit from our natural inclinations. And then we can make room for our teammates to shine when their tendencies become more valuable contributions.

A CONTROL OVERCOMING HIS BIOLOGY TO APPRECIATE AND SELL BETTER TO AUTHORITIES

"I am a salesperson and Authorities have been the bane of my existence as for as long as I can remember. It's a momentum question. I like a lot of forward momentum. I like thinking through to how the result of a deal can positively impact their business. I like "what ifs" and I like to spitball with my clients and dream and say, 'Let's put a man on the moon!'

"But the natural starting point for an Authority always seems to be to focus solely on what could go wrong.

Continued...

They want everything so detailed and so planned out and worry about everything. They've just always seemed like roadblocks to me during the deal cycle. So, in the past, I've bulldozed them, focused instead on their partners or their boss, or just moved on from them if they were the only person in the transaction because I didn't see them as a buyer. Obviously none of those approaches got me very far.

"What I've discovered through the Market Force material is that Authorities have a really great place in the deal cycle. They ask really great questions, pointing to things that could go wrong, giving us the chance to avoid them. Over time, I have really learned to embrace their perspective, not to brush them off, but rather to say, 'OK, let's think about that for a minute . . . what *does* this button do if we push it?' It's gotten to the point now that I actually want an Authority on the other side because it gives me comfort that when a deal moves forward, it will have a better outcome. To say this Market Force training has helped my relationship with Authorities would be a huge understatement."

MAKING PROGRESS

The second 50/50 category is called "Making Progress." Making progress in our daily business lives means *balancing thinking and acting*. One without the other can cause us problems. Too much time spent planning can make things feel stagnant and cause us to miss out on real opportunities. In contrast, too much action without a plan can be the source of wasted time and resources.

As it relates to Styles, pressure is the trigger that determines our primary response. Two of the Styles will be more inclined to "think before they act" and the other two to "act before they think." Neither approach is right or wrong, and both are clearly necessary. Awareness of the differences allows us to continue making progress, even under pressure.

The 50/50 for "Making Progress" looks like this:

Controls and Authorities tend to **THINK AND THEN ACT** under pressure. They typically want time "to plan" out a situation before they're comfortable moving forward. However, these two Styles tend to focus on different things:

- Due to a Control's focus on the future, they are more likely to spend time considering the significance of the situation and calculating the next move, exhibiting more of their offensive nature.

- Operating from the point of view of history, an Authority tends to review what has happened in order to determine how we actually wound up in this situation.

Conversely, Influences and Powers tend to be **ACT FIRST, THEN THINK** Styles, meaning their nature is to respond quickly, then later determine if their actions seem to be working and if not, to adjust as they go. Here is how these two Styles differ from one another:

- Operating within their "right now" time frame, Influences have an urge to just "get going" on things. Standing around (or even strategizing what to do) can feel like a huge waste of time.

- Due to a Power's focus on structure and their preference for a time frame of the next 90 days, Powers feel most comfortable jumping on things that need to get done as opposed to looking for something new to initiate.

It is important to acknowledge that these natural inclinations do not prevent any of the Styles from engaging appropriately in a given situation. *Everyone thinks and acts.* This distinction simply signifies that each Style's natural priority under pressure will be either to be a planner or to be a doer. They will always come around to the other one after the pressure has subsided.

50/50S SUMMARY

The 50/50s we presented paired together different sets of Styles. The outcome of those 50/50s provides one of the best opportunities to use the Styles map in a topographical way. Doing so will illuminate the core contribution that each Style brings to their team and what they become known for:

CONTROLS

A Control is offensive like an Influence and thought-oriented like an Authority. They are regularly thinking about what the future holds. Controls have an innate desire to design that next new idea that will revolutionize the direction of the team. This means a Control's core contribution is for the **VISION**.

INFLUENCES

An Influence is offensive in nature like a Control, but with an orientation toward action like a Power. Influences possess a natural inclination for discovering and moving quickly on real-time opportunities for growth, so they often like to start new projects or new relationships. This means an Influence's core contribution is for **VELOCITY**.

POWERS

A Power is defensive in nature like an Authority, and then they are action-oriented like an Influence. This means their attention is on the building of processes that allow their teams to dig in and deliver on all of the ideas and promises that have been made. Therefore, a Power's core contribution to a team is for the design of **STRUCTURE**.

AUTHORITIES

An Authority is defensive like a Power, but then they have a thought orientation like a Control. The result is that they have the most naturally reflective and analytical Style. Authorities take great pride in their ability to evaluate every detail of a project to find a better way to make things work. This makes their core contribution **QUALITY**.

As we look at the core contributions all together now, we see that vision, velocity, structure, and quality are critical to building a high-performance team.

Next, we wrap up the Styles distinctions by looking at how the four behavioral Styles work to build trust.

CHAPTER 8

BUILDING TRUST

"Relationships survive on trust, and if that is broken at any point, it's pretty much the end of the relationship. Besides, the inability to communicate leads to problems."

—Yuvraj Singh

In business you can only sell to the level of trust that you have with another person. Sadly, not all salespeople operate with the same high level of integrity that you do. Not all salespeople care about their customers as much as you do. And, as a result, we have all suffered varying degrees of negative sales experiences in the past. We've been lied to, we've been manipulated, and we've been taken advantage of. Being treated this way feels terrible, and it has eroded our trust in salespeople and in the sales process in general.

This is a shame, but it is also the price of admission in the sales game. As a successful salesperson, you already know that you have to overcome this implicit bias every time you establish a new relationship. You also know that this one factor can become an incredible advantage for you. Because once you are able to overcome that negative perception, you clearly differentiate yourself from the pack. The more trust you build with someone, the stronger that relationship becomes, and the more value you can create from it over time.

But did you know that not everyone builds trust the same way? Your Style massively impacts *how* you build trust. This is true for you, and it is also true for everyone you seek to build trust with. There are two ways that we build trust, and without awareness, you will always intuitively follow your own preference—which actually works for only about 50 percent of the population. It's the other 50 percent of the population that poses the problem. You see, they prefer to build trust in a completely different way than you do.

This single discrepancy causes you to miss out on half the sales opportunities you pursue!

The good news is that the Diamond Rule helps you to be able to see this difference in people and provides you with the flexibility to effectively build trust with them the way *that feels most natural to them.* As long as you are able to remain focused on the needs of the other person, this one trick will help you double the number of people you are able to build trust with. And, of course, it all comes back to your identity.

ONE KEY ELEMENT FOR TRUST

Earlier, we distinguished that the *measurement* of your identity is the assessment that people have about how much value *you are able to create for them* combined with *how much they trust you.*

It is the second component of identity that we will dig into now: trust. We know that we all agree that trust in business is essential to getting things done. So, given its importance, let's help you gain some insight into what trust is all about.

Let's start here: Trust is not something that's earned *nor* is it something that's given. Trust is actually built, and it is built over time, and it needs to be reinforced regularly. Trust is comprised of two very specific elements that we refer to as sincerity and competence. Even if your language for these is a little bit different, most people agree with these major categories.

When we talk about sincerity, we mean that part of trust when you are considering whether you like someone, whether you feel they are being honest with you, whether they appear to be authentic, and whether you believe they will have your back if things get tough.

When we talk about competence, we mean that other part of the instinctual trust equation when you are looking at whether you believe someone has the ability to do what they say they can do, whether you think they have the necessary skill set to do the task, and whether you feel they will follow through and be dependable over time.

Make no mistake, everybody needs both sincerity and competence—you won't trust somebody unless both elements are present.

It has been found that 80 percent of how we judge other people comes down to just these two factors.[8]

For instance, if you meet somebody who seems to be really skillful and accomplished, but you find out that they're stabbing you in the back, then they lack the sincerity you need to fully trust them. Likewise, if you meet somebody who is really nice and friendly and who is excited to work with you, but you determine they won't be able to get the job done, you may like them but you won't feel like you can trust that person because the competence element is lacking.

The key takeaway here is that to trust somebody, you need to feel secure they are *both sincere and competent.* When both of those elements exist, you will say you trust that person.

AN INFLUENCE ADJUSTING HER APPROACH TO BUILDING MORE TRUST WITH CONTROLS AND AUTHORITIES

"As an Influence, I am very sincerity-based when it comes to building trust. Likeability is such a strong driver for me. When a client takes a sincere approach with me, that really helps me trust them because it just feels so natural. I can't get enough of it!

"But Market Force has taught me that not all of my clients like to start off our meetings with a "get-to-know-you" conversation. And, in fact, many get turned off by it.

Continued...

---

8. https://harvardmagazine.com/2010/11/the-psyche-on-automatic

> I've learned that the competence-based Styles, like Controls and Authorities, want more of a business-first conversation or a 'Hey, read this and get back to me' approach. While that doesn't feel natural to me, I've gotten so much more comfortable with it over time, because I can feel that's what they need to trust me.
>
> "Now I challenge myself to start competence-first with potential clients who are Controls or Authorities and see how quickly I can get them to the sincerity conversation. It's a fun game actually!"

BUILDING TRUST FOLLOWS TWO DISTINCT PATHS

As we now know, trust is comprised of two key elements, sincerity *and* competence, and both must be present for trust to occur. We also know that trust must be built in a specific order to work, meaning that one of those elements has to be confirmed before the other is even considered. So, which do you suppose comes first, competence or sincerity?

Well, of course, the rank order depends on your Style! Some Styles want competence first, sincerity second, while others want sincerity first, competence second. Remember, we all need both, but we tend to build trust in different orders. And we won't even consider the second trait until we're clear about the first.

A SALES TEAM WORKING TOGETHER TO BUILD MORE CLIENT TRUST

"Once my team and I realized that there really are two different orders in which people build trust, it created an incredible awareness for us to pay attention to the little things with our clients. I'm a Power and my two associates are Influences, so we are all on the sincerity side of the equation, and we laugh now about how we always used to start our meetings with clients the same way. We would just naturally gravitate to the other sincerity-based people in the room, not even noticing that the Controls and Authorities were getting impatient with us. Total blindspot! And, when we would finally get around to start talking business, there would be this moment where it felt like the gears were kind of grinding a bit with the competence-based folks because of course, we were not building any sort of trust with them.

"Now we have learned to realize that we should probably jump into talking about business first for some of our competence-based clients, or at least get there faster if there is a mix of Styles in the room. Truthfully, we've had a lot of our meetings start differently because of our awareness. We now gauge whether the other parties want to jump straight into the presentation and go through the competence side of the equation first or talk a little bit more about each other and what's important to us to build that sincerity base. It's been great for us as a team to have this awareness."

Trust is another one of those factors that splits the map right in half with Controls and Authorities on one side and Influences and Powers on the other.

The primary trust concern for Controls and Authorities is **COMPETENCE**. Until these Styles have a solid feeling on the competence side of the ledger, they won't even bother considering whether or not that person is sincere. However, even though these two Styles are competence-based, *how they assess another person's competence* differs.

- A Control's primary trust concern focuses on the **COMPETENCE OF OTHERS**. Interestingly though, Controls only believe you to be competent to the extent that *you see them as competent*. They need to know that you can think on their level and that you get their ideas.

- An Authority's primary concern is for **THEIR OWN COMPETENCE**. No matter how smart an Authority is, they're often insecure about being seen by others as not able to understand the topic at hand. Anyone who may reveal this shortcoming poses a genuine threat to them and is definitely *not to be trusted*.

AN INFLUENCE WINNING OVER A CONTROL PROSPECT BY FOLLOWING THE DIAMOND RULE

"A few years ago, I was really struggling to make a connection with a prospect who, despite my best efforts, was elusive and notoriously difficult to build a relationship with. This was an account I really wanted because

Continued...

I knew we could provide them with great value, and it could be a great client for us. But I was getting nowhere and felt I was annoying him. He was especially short with me in email communications.

"Around this time, I began learning Market Force Styles. As an Influence, I quickly realized that I had been applying the Golden Rule to this guy, who is a Control, trying to get him to like me by focusing over and over on sincerity first! As I began applying the Diamond Rule, I noticed a massive turn-around in my relationship with him, and it happened quickly.

"The first thing I did was switch to short, clear, and to-the-point calls avoiding any "noise" or "chitchat." Second, when sending him emails, I only sent high-level summaries instead of my typical long and rambling updates, which I'm sure were selectively or rarely read. Next, I was mindful to acknowledge his "vast" industry experience (his competence) in order to gain a more personal rapport with him over time. And I figured out where he wanted to increase his identity, which came up one time about how one of his principal concerns was how he looked to his CFO (an Authority) in terms of adding value to the business. To help him there, I made sure to highlight bottom-line returns for him to pass on internally, which allowed him to quickly grow his identity with his CFO.

"As a result of following the Diamond Rule, he went from being a potential client who ranted at me for wasting his time to becoming a long-term client who now refers to me as his friend. I have secured much larger assignments over time, and at the time of this writing, I am about to close over $1 million in gross revenue over the past two years from projects awarded by this client."

On the other end of this trust continuum, Influences and Powers have a primary trust concern for **SINCERITY**. Until they believe someone to be honest and sincere, they have no interest in evaluating whether or not that person is competent. Again, between these two sincerity-based Styles, *how they assess sincerity* differs.

- For Influences, their primary trust concern is for **THEIR OWN SINCERITY**. Their attention can rapidly bounce from one thing to another, causing them to sometimes question their own motives. Since relationships are so important to them, it is critical that they are seen as likable by other people, which can have them be overly excited about projects at the beginning or overly apologetic if there has been a breakdown along the way.

- Powers are interested in the **SINCERITY OF OTHERS**. Powers love to build teams and get things done, so their first trust concern is determining whether or not they feel you will work and collaborate well with them. So, whereas Influences are concerned with *likeability*, Powers focus more on *workability*. They want to know that you are willing to roll up your sleeves, work hard, and get things done. Those attributes go a long way with Powers.

THE POWER OF BUILDING TRUST IN THE RIGHT ORDER WITH PEOPLE

"I've learned that if the person in front of me is a competency-based person, I'm going to need to lead with a certain language pattern around facts and analysis and

Continued...

data that helps regulate the brain and allows for the pre-frontal cortex to process. By contrast, if I'm dealing with somebody who is sincerity-based, they're going to want to have the touchy-feely stories first and understand the color, the dynamics, the culture, and the feeling of our relationship. For me personally, in the absence of aware-ness, my brain automatically starts to distrust you if you haven't met my sincerity need first. And so already I'm pigeonholing others if I am not careful and aware of my own biology. The most important thing I do now is first understand how to approach new people I meet. By just simply looking for sincerity or competency needs, I feel I have become much more efficient and effective at creat-ing initial rapport with others."

With the understanding that trust is something that we build with each other, and depending on someone's Style, it is either built on com-petence-first or sincerity-first, you can begin modifying your approach with others based on what they need rather than what is important to you. What's critical to remember is that the secondary consideration doesn't play a role at all until the first concern is satisfied.

Here's a review of the 10 Styles distinctions:

- 3 Survival Characteristics

- 4 Desires

- 2 50/50s

- 1 Key for Building Trust

In the next section, we'll look at the process of mining for diamonds. Diamonds are truly valuable and you won't just find them laying around ready to pick up. You have to go searching for them and you have to uncover where they are hidden. The M.I.N.E. approach will best prepare you to apply the Diamond Rule.

MINING FOR DIAMONDS (THE WHAT)

CHAPTER 9

WHAT DOES IT MEAN TO M.I.N.E. FOR DIAMONDS?

"Be a diamond. Flourish under pressure."

— Maureen Joyce Connolly

Remember, Diamonds are mined 90 percent less than gold annually. And compared to Platinum, if they maintain clarity and are cut correctly, they can be upwards of 10 times more valuable.

In sales, this means that you have a chance to be in the top producers if you will apply the Diamond Rule.

This section explores WHAT you have to do to apply the Styles framework in order to make it all happen.

In the next four chapters, we'll break down our acronym for M.I.N.E.:

- **M** for Mindset

- **I** for Identify

- **N** for Neutralize

- **E** for Empathize

But first a quick story.

Both Travis and Stan are former attorneys. Interestingly, when discussing this section of the book, they stumbled upon a learning they both had between the first and second semesters of law school.

When they both started law school, their assumption was that they were about to learn the law. Makes sense, right? Seems logical enough.

With that perspective, they both diligently took copious notes, created study groups, bought commercial outlines, and prepped for first semester exams by taking in as much law on the respective topics as possible.

Then came Fall exams. For each class, they were given four hours to answer five questions. Their three-ring binders filled with about 6 inches of documents per course were distilled down to a handful of questions.

In that moment, both realized they were not learning the law. Truthfully, they both thought at the time they were about to fail out of law school!

Instead, they were being taught to think like lawyers. Yes, they were learning some of the law on different subjects (like contracts, property, torts, and civil procedure), but more importantly, they were being shown a new way of thinking through and spotting issues, applying critical thinking, and drawing conclusions. The process follows an acronym known as **FIRAC**. It stands for **F**acts, **I**ssue, **R**ule, **A**nalysis, and **C**onclusion. Here's a summary of each:

> **Facts** - understanding the situation
>
> **Issue** - finding the main question or issue from the facts
>
> **Rule** - finding how similar issues have been handled in the past
>
> **Analysis** - looking at how this case applies for or against past precedent
>
> **Conclusion** - moving forward and making a judgment based on the analysis

This process is consistent with learning Styles and understanding how to act upon that understanding.

The purpose of mining is to teach you how to think differently. Viewing the world through the Diamond Rule is very different than just learning tips and techniques for how to close a deal. It's a whole new way of thinking.

Back to law school.

By the time second semester rolls around, every law student changes their approach to taking notes, studying, and preparing for exams. It's all about thinking dynamically—thinking about how you will deal with any given situation based on the facts at hand.

Again, this is a perfect analogy to mining for Diamonds!

Using Styles does not mean that you change the content of what you intend to deliver—things like the business issues of prospecting for new clients, getting deal points agreed to, and working on delivering a product or service. All of these things still need to happen and using Styles does not make them less relevant.

Instead, using Styles changes the packaging around the content— things like the order in which you present things, where you meet, and what you emphasize first, second, and third. When you adjust the packaging around your content to account for Styles, that's mining for Diamonds, that's living the Diamond Rule.

When you are focused on playing the game of business like a champion, you begin asking yourself questions like:

- How do I make a great first impression on a Control?

- How do I negotiate a win-win with an Influence?

- How do manage a relationship with a Power over time?

- How should I follow up after a project is over with an Authority?

Questions like these make all the difference. They put you in the right frame of mind going into meetings with other people. And, they allow you to work on adjusting your behavior in a way that relieves pressure on others in the game of business.

Instead, most people intuitively focus on themselves, asking, "What works for me in this situation?"

AN EYE-OPENING MOMENT FOR AN INFLUENCE WITH A CONTROL

"We've always been taught to believe that we should treat others the way that we would like to be treated, you know—the Golden Rule. But with Market Force, it was the first time I realized that there's actually a better way. That if we're able to manage against our biology when we're feeling pressure and treat people *the way they want to be treated* in those moments, we will actually be much more successful. That was such a new way of thinking for me.

"But here's the thing. It's not so easy to know how to treat someone the way they want to be treated unless you have a good sense of who they are and what's important to them. Through Market Force, I have been able to really understand other people much more easily than I ever thought possible.

"One of the greatest examples for me is a relationship I have with a senior executive at my biggest client. I really enjoy spending time with him. Before learning about the Diamond Rule, anytime we would talk, since I'm an Influence, I would always make sure to start with some kind of social connection. I would talk to him about things

Continued...

I did on the weekend or what I was doing with my family and ask him about the same. It turns out that he, as a Control, actually had little interest in that conversation, at least not at first.

"It was fascinating for me to learn what was truly really important to him. Looking back it seems so obvious now! His whole office was arranged such that he didn't have any guest chairs around his desk, instead they were pushed over in the corner around a small coffee table. That should have been a pretty good indication to me what was important to him. But I never gave it any thought.

"So, I began to change my tune. I started coming in and getting down to business right away. I led with updates and feedback, answered his questions, and just followed his lead on what he wanted to talk about. Once we started having the conversations he wanted to have, he and I became much closer, not necessarily because our personal bond got much stronger but because he feels more validated and values the fact that I understand who he is and what he is looking for.

"It's funny because now I actually notice how others around him interact with him how I used to do. I can see the frustration on his face in a way that is just painful. I'm so glad he doesn't look at me like that anymore."

To avoid falling into the Golden Rule trap, here are your four "What" questions (your Mining Checklist) for applying the Diamond Rule moving forward.

1. [Mindset] What Style am I dealing with?

2. [Identify] What is the situation?

3. [Neutralize] What do I need to do to set aside my Style?

4. [Empathize] What are my tactics?

The following four chapters will dig into this checklist in greater detail. We'd recommend that over the next ten days, you find three interactions with other people to apply the Mining Checklist. When you do, you will find that your awareness around the importance of treating people according to their Style will greatly increase and that the game of business will become even more fun.

Let us walk you through two examples involving first meetings:

An Influence meets an Authority:

1. [M] **What Style am I dealing with?** I think he/she is an Authority.

2. [I] **What is the situation?** It's a first meeting, and I want to make a great first impression.

3. [N] **What do I need to do to set aside my Style?** I'm an Influence. I need to manage my impatience for wanting this meeting to go faster.

4. [E] **What are my tactics?** I should prepare more data than I am comfortable with, and I need to send it over beforehand.

Your tactics will come together by employing what you have learned. For example, you know that an Authority has a competence-based preference for trust, so that could inform where you meet (their office). And you know that Authorities have a primary time frame of the past, so introducing case studies of past performance early on in the conversation should be helpful. While there are more tools you could employ, using just those two should give you a nice starting point for your tactics.

Next, let's look at a similar example, but this time from the perspective of how an Authority might approach the same situation with an Influence:

1. [M] **What Style am I dealing with?** I think he/she is an Influence.

2. 2. [I] **What is the situation?** It's a first meeting, and I want to make a great first impression.

3. 3. [N] **What do I need to do to set aside my Style?** I'm an Authority. I need to manage my focus on the deal and prep myself to connect before I get into the details.

4. 4. [E] **What are my tactics?** I should prepare to be relaxed and look to transition to the deal conversation only when they are ready.

Once again, using the tools you know, you can begin to put together your tactics. Starting again with trust, you know an Influence has a Sincerity-based approach to trust, so maybe you want to offer to meet at a restaurant or coffee shop, and remember to try to open the conversation in more of a personal manner. Once again, just using these two tools, you are able to zero in on what feels like a nice starting point for how you can package yourself to reduce pressure and make a great first impression on an Influence.

In the end, following the Diamond Rule is easy to say, but hard to do. Reading through the following four chapters will give you more confidence to make it happen.

Let's start with **Mindset**.

CHAPTER 10

MINDSET

"If my mind can conceive it and my heart can believe it - then I can achieve it."

— Muhammad Ali

Succeeding in mining for diamonds is as much about our mindset as it is the Mining Checklist. We've found two key elements to achieving the Diamond Rule mindset:

1. Think of sales as relationships, not transactions **and**

2. Approach relationships in a judgment-free perspective

Let's look at each of these core pillars.

RELATIONSHIPS NOT TRANSACTIONS

"I don't like salespeople" or "I don't do sales" are statements we hear a lot in our daily lives. When you want to describe someone that you experience as creepy, you call them a "used car salesperson."

Many people claim to "hate sales" or "hate being sold to." This is understandable. Nobody wants to be sold to. It can feel like the salesperson is "up to something" or trying to get us to do something we don't want to do.

Most average or below average salespeople are thinking of their clients as transactions, or worse, as conquests. Yuck, it's no wonder why those experiences feel so bad. In those situations, the salesperson is focused on their own needs, which is to push things along in order to make money.

Honestly, that's not even a Golden Rule approach!

In order to become a Diamond Rule salesperson, it is imperative that you move away from techniques that move the transaction and instead focus more on reducing pressure for the other person.

Doing this will improve the relationship, not just at the point of sale, but all the way through the engagement.

Someone who mines for Diamonds is thinking as much about how to help the person once the closing happens as they are about making a deal. That's why we want you applying the mining process all the way through the sales cycle—from prospecting to following up after a successful project.

All touchpoints are important when you look through the lens of a relationship and not just a transaction.

JUDGMENT-FREE PERSPECTIVE

This might sound strange at first, but the idea is that others are responding to their biology in terms of reacting to pressure. So making assessments or judgments about how people are responding to different pressure-filled situations is a bit unfair.

Consider the idea of being judgment-neutral when you meet with someone for the first time. As you look around, as you speak with them, look to avoid bringing in anything that sounds like your opinion of them. In the words of the late Muhammad Ali, "Real magic in relationships means an absence of judgment of others."

Stay at a high level just watching their behavior and looking for pressure points. This mindset will enable you to avoid setting your own traps along the way.

If we look at each Style from that non-judgment lens, here are the overviews you can bring into every conversation with the different Styles moving forward:

CONTROLS

A Control generally is seen as competent, big picture-oriented, and focused on achieving a strategy. They are the Style typically most focused on new ideas and perspectives about whether new projects have the makings for success. When Controls are performing at their highest and best, they are socializing their ideas by using Influence traits and not attempting to force their ideas onto their team or others. A team without a Control may tend to lose its conviction and direction, which means that others will begin to complain that there is no clear vision for where the team is going.

INFLUENCES

An Influence is usually seen as intuitive and people-oriented and often is seen as the most outgoing person on the team. Theirs is the Style generally most focused on getting people engaged and excited about new projects. When Influences are performing at their highest and best, they are not only getting projects started but also bringing enough discipline to make sure the projects are being completed, even if done so by teammates. A team without an Influence may tend to struggle with creating new relationships in the marketplace, which can be the lifeblood of any organization's success.

POWERS

A Power is typically seen as reliable and dependable, someone you can trust to work very hard and get tasks done. Powers are often the most loyal and trustworthy as well as easiest to work with on a day-in, day-out basis. When performing at their highest and best, Powers hold the team together and act more discerning about priorities to make sure that the most important things are getting done, not just that the team is following a routine. A team without a Power will struggle with producing all of their work in a timely fashion. Powers have the natural predisposition to grind out more work than all of the other Styles.

HELPING A CONTROL CONNECT BETTER WITH A POWER

"I recently met with one of my senior salespeople who was really frustrated that he wasn't getting anywhere with one of the bigger opportunities in his pipeline. He was super motivated to get that deal done but was feeling stuck. I listened to him describe the opportunity, who the prospect was, the state of the relationship, and how he had been approaching it. He was clear that he and the prospect weren't on the same page, but he couldn't figure out what was going wrong.

"Because I know Market Force and am familiar with the Diamond Rule, it was pretty obvious to me what the problem was. I explained to him that he and the prospect were different Styles and were looking for different things out of their discussions. I explained that he was a Control and she was a Power and that the way he was presenting wasn't clicking with her because of that. I said, 'Look, you're talking about all these big-picture, conceptual ideas and strategic ways in which you can solve her problems way out in the future, and that's just not how she thinks about things. She's looking for you to collaborate with her in real time on what the plan is and she wants to know how you two plan to make measurable progress quickly.' I let him know that Powers are the most practical of the Styles and want their problems solved within the next 90 days at the latest. Anything beyond that seems too far out there to be useful to them and frankly, it kind of sounds to them that you're afraid of doing the work. My suggestion to him was to take his grand ideas and boil them down

Continued...

into bite-sized, actionable chunks, and then present them to her as a roadmap with checklists.

"Sure enough the next time we met, he shared that he sat down with this prospect, followed this new approach, which had them collaborate "elbow-to-elbow," and now the two of them had started building a much better connection. He said to me with great relief, 'We are finally getting somewhere.' "

AUTHORITIES

An Authority is typically seen as extremely competent though quiet, reserved, and introspective. They will often be your go-to person for things such as research, details, evidence, facts, and numbers. When Authorities are performing at their highest and best, they will look at their research but also will be passionate and show conviction about making decisions. A team without an Authority will struggle with matters of compliance and quality control, which can erode a team's identity in the marketplace over time.

AN AUTHORITY BECOMING MORE COMFORTABLE USING THE DIAMOND RULE

"I'm an Authority and when I first started playing with the Diamond Rule (and Styles), I felt sometimes that I

Continued...

was manipulating people, which made me uncomfortable. Integrity in relationships is really important to me. But now I have become convinced that's not what it's about at all. It's just meeting people where they are when there is pressure in the environment so that we can accomplish our mutual goals. I now see the Diamond Rule as one of the most respectful ways of interacting with people, which is a big change for me to say the least. I've really come to learn that when I recognize my Control clients for their ideas, or listen to my Influence clients and allow them to have their excitement, they become more comfortable, and they like working with me more. When I provide checklists to my Power clients or my Authority clients (who are like me) get their data, it makes them happy. Once I finally understood that the point of the Diamond Rule is to help people feel better, it became a no-brainer for me. I have found that when I focus more on empathy, it just seems easier to break down any initial barrier and relieve the stress so that we can get past them to achieve a common goal."

So mining for Diamonds begins by starting from a judgment-free zone and going into relationships.

From there, we can focus completely on how to Identify the other person.

CHAPTER 11

IDENTIFY

"The real voyage of discovery consists not in seeking new landscapes, but in having new eyes."

– Marcel Proust

As we move into relationships in a judgment-free mindset, we can now turn our attention to the mining checklist. Playing by the Diamond Rule requires us to treat others how they want to be treated, so the question quickly becomes, "But how do I know how other people want to be treated?"

That is a great question. In fact, that is the first question that everyone asks as they begin to walk the Diamond Rule path. Simply becoming curious about and putting your attention on what another person needs is following the Diamond Rule. Remember the words of Andre Agassi. He said, "You can't problem solve unless you have the ability or the empathy to perceive all that's around you. The more you understand what the problem is through other people's lens, the more you can solve for people, in life and in business."

TWO THINGS TO KNOW FOR IMPLEMENTING THE DIAMOND RULE

"So I focus in on only two things when I follow the Diamond Rule. First, I determine which part of trust is more important for the other person—do they have a primary concern for competence or for sincerity? This one piece of data informs so much about what to do next. The second area of focus is which time frame feels most comfortable for them to operate in—do they like looking at the past? Hanging out in the present? Are they more comfortable in the short-term or the long-term future? As soon as I gather these two pieces of information, I feel like I know a lot about them, and I really feel I can speak to them in language and in ways that make a difference."

You don't need to know how someone wants to be treated because they will tell you in one of three ways:

1. **Through observing them**

   Since most people are always following the Golden Rule, that means that they are usually treating others how they themselves want to be treated. So, simply mimic their behavior and language back to them.

2. **By asking them**

   Don't assume, ask! If there are a couple of different approaches that you could take with a prospect, don't try to read their mind. Ask which they prefer, or if there's another way that you hadn't thought of. The goal is to build identity, and the identity you want to build is someone who cares about what is important to them.

3. **By predicting needs based on their Style**

   People's behavior under some level of pressure is predictable because it is associated with one of the four survival strategies. Their actions are intended to reduce the pressure they feel. Styles allows you to predict where the other person may feel extra pressure. It allows you to anticipate and avoid those triggers.

This last point is a true challenge. Getting into the right mindset and focusing on the needs of the other person is the most important element. But, if we are to get good at predicting needs based on Styles, we have to dig into how to identify others before we worry about changing our behavior to address their needs. The good news is that once you have the awareness, people are tipping their hand all the time. Like anything else we learn, getting good at Styles identification takes time.

We are on a journey, a journey to following the Diamond Rule in the game of business. And the next step on our journey requires us to turn outward and begin to focus more on how to spot other Styles in the wild (which will take practice), and then we can learn to adjust our behavior to relieve pressure for those other Styles.

The first thing to note is that Styles Identification is not as easy with humans as it is with other animals in the animal kingdom— and that's because other animals are endowed with a physical manifestation of their Style and their Survival Strategy. For example, it makes sense that a rhinoceros with a big horn Dictates when it feels threatened or how birds got their wings in order to fly and Migrate quickly away from the pressure or how a buffalo has a heavy winter coat as part of its body in order to Tolerate the risk of winter or how a tortoise has a hard shell for when it pulls back from the danger and Hibernates. Unlike these animals, humans all (generally) look the same without physical manifestations of our respective Styles.

To get good at Styles identification takes time and practice. Let's get you going.

Three Prerequisites for Styles Identification

There are three prerequisites that you must do in order to optimize your Styles identification capabilities:

1. Ask Open Ended Questions

As easy as this sounds, asking open-ended questions is critical to Styles Identification. When you ask an open-ended question, you create a touch of pressure for the other person to fill the space. Think about it this way—there are no magical questions that will make Styles identification easy; instead, you have to ask open-ended questions and learn to listen closely to what the other person focuses on—what is important to them. The better your open-ended questions and the more you are listening, the better the chance you have at identifying their Style.

2. Look as Well as Listen

It might be of interest to you that the more you practice Styles Identification, the more you will realize that it is not just what people say that matters but also how they create the environment all around themselves and in their lives. Looking at things like how they dress, how their office looks, etc. will provide clues along the way in Styles Identification. Sometimes the environment can speak volumes. For example, if you walk into an office filled with lots of certificates and degrees on the wall, it would be a safe first guess to say that person has a competence-base to their Style, meaning their Style is Authority or Control. So being aware of what the other person has around them is a great way to read signs even before you hear them speak.

3. Be Positive

As it relates to Styles Identification, there is an inherent fear about being wrong. And this makes sense—none of us want to get something wrong! However, it is important to understand that Styles Identification is art as much as science, so stay in a positive mindset even if you are struggling a bit. Just keep doing the work by looking and listening. The ongoing question you can ask yourself is: "What Style would do that?" Continuing to check in will enable you to see the other person's core Style at some point, especially when that other person feels pressure.

By keeping these three prerequisites in mind, your journey to competence in Styles Identification will go much easier. And the quicker you get someone else's Style, the sooner you can begin relieving their pressure.

MAKING THE DIAMOND RULE A PRACTICE

"I tell people all of the time that if they want to get value out of the Diamond Rule, they have to put it into practice. I acknowledge that it's going to be a task at first. It is going to be something that you have to remind yourself of regularly and you have to catch yourself when you get triggered. It's definitely a mental thing that you have to do for a while. But then, without even realizing it, it becomes a habit. You start doing it without even knowing it. It even becomes natural to do when you are feeling pressure, just because it works so well. At least that's the way it's worked for me over the years.

"My process is to learn through listening, first to my own biology and settle that down, and then to the other person and what they need. After that, I act and see how the person responds, then listen again and adjust. It's like a rinse and repeat cycle, you just keep doing it to get better results. Because once you really listen to the other person, you go, 'Oh I think this person's a Power' and then you act in a way for that works for a Power. And then you pay attention to how they respond. Does it seem to be working? If not, then maybe they're not a Power, and I make my next guess and try again. The important part is to try and keep trying. In my view, it's all about actually doing something with the information you have at the time.

"I'll be honest, at first, I was a bit scared because it was different, and I didn't want to offend people. I worried about getting it wrong. It took me a while, but now I'm just acting on what I see and hear, listening and act-

Continued...

ing, and changing my actions based on the results that I'm getting. There are only four Styles, so if you stick with the program, you will get there eventually. Most people never do because they aren't thinking this way. The Diamond Rule doesn't solve every problem in the world, but it makes things a lot easier and less ugly and painful to get through, which is the goal."

Now, let's dig into the distinctions you focus on specifically for Styles identification.

THE STYLES IDENTIFICATION METHODOLOGY

To help you close the gap toward competence with Styles Identification, we offer an easy-to-follow three-step Styles Identification methodology that will ultimately become your mental scoresheet. This means that while you are speaking with someone, you will need to be running this methodology in your mind and looking for clues.

The methodology employs three primary distinctions for you to look and listen for:

1. Primary Trust Concern

Simply stated, the number one tool for Styles Identification is to look for the other person's primary trust concern—competence or sincerity.

As you know, everyone needs both of these to assign trust, but the question is: which one do they appear to want first? The answer to this question will narrow your inquiry to two Styles instead of four. You'll remember that Controls and Authorities will want competence first, while on the other hand, Influences and Powers will want sincerity first.

To identify the primary trust concern, requires both listening and looking:

- In conversation, the competence-based Styles will presumably be business focused, want to discuss facts and data first, and will want to get to the point quickly. Conversely, the sincerity-based Styles may want to relate and connect (often through storytelling) before they want to talk business.

- In decoration, you may notice that the competence-based Styles have very work-related work spaces with credibility-oriented décor, including all of their degrees and certificates up on their walls. On the other side, the sincerity-based Styles tend to have more expressive décor in their work space, often times with a number of trinkets and photographs.

2. Position on the Field

Position on the field relates back to whether someone is more of an offensive player or a defensive player. As you are speaking with someone, notice what they focus on and what type of language they are using.

- **OFFENSIVE** - The offensive Styles, Controls & Influences, tend to focus more on how they want to start new things, on new ideas and possibilities and, in regard to their language, their tone tends to be more about what we should or could do if we had more time, money, people . . . fill in the blank.

- **DEFENSIVE** - Defensive Styles, Powers & Authorities, on the other hand, tend to focus on how many things they are trying to get done, doing things well, and what's in the way of their workload. Defensive players, in regard to their language and tone, tend to focus on what we have to do, the deadlines we need to stick to, and what we should have done in the past.

Because these two distinctions split the map 50/50, they are giving you a great jumping off point for Styles Identification without putting additional pressure on you to pick one Style. Just move through those two 50/50s and see where you land.

Then, use the third distinction to double-check yourself before you move into action.

AN APPROACH TO IDENTIFYING THE STYLE OF EXECUTIVES

"This is an approach I take that's specific to working with executives who have a broader perspective of the whole business. I think the most effective way to identify someone's Style is to play with the distinction called 50/50s, where you divide the Styles map in half two different ways, instead of trying to figure it all out at once. I first listen for the competency or sincerity concern, you know, how people like to build trust, and then I try to figure out if they are more comfortable on offense or defense.

"When I meet a new executive who is a potential client, I love to ask, 'So tell me, what is your company's secret sauce?' If the prospect is more competence-based, their response is more about a strategic approach or a commercial competitive advantage. If they are sincerity-

Continued...

based, the answer is usually more about the people and how the team works together, or maybe even their approaches with their clients.

"To determine offense or defense, the next question I ask is, 'Would you mind telling me something you are most proud of from your career?' Offensive people usually describe something new for their company, something they started or invented. It's more about the idea. Defensive players tend to talk about things they persevered through or the work they did. It's more about accomplishing things.

"Other open-ended questions I like to ask are, 'Tell me what has us sitting down here today?' or 'Tell me what would be the most valuable thing we could have covered today when you walk out the door?' The most important thing is to get them talking, and then I listen for whether they are leading with competency or sincerity. Are they asking for a relationship, or are they asking for knowledge? And it's critical that I never lead with something about me. I try not to say anything about me until I ask a few questions so that I can provide them with something in their own language pattern back to them. Basically, I try to be a chameleon. It's still me every time, but it's the version of me that's the most respectful and genuine for the ears in front of me."

3. How You Experience Them

This distinction takes us all of the way back to the beginning of the Styles conversation— namely that the game of business is about identity.

So here you are looking for how someone else is positioning their identity with you along with their mannerisms. If we break this down by Style:

- **CONTROLS** – A Control will often position themselves as in charge (or if not in charge, "I should be in charge")—so as a **DIRECTOR**. They will be measured and pensive, often looking out a window and thinking.

- **INFLUENCES** - An Influence will position themselves around relationships—all the people they know and if you know the same people—so they will feel more like a **CONNECTOR** or Facilitator. Plus their manner will feel more restless or energetic, almost impatient.

- **POWERS** – A Power will position themselves as very busy and indispensable to their team's success—meaning that they will come across to you as the **BUILDER**. Along the way, they will be pleasant and more even-keeled or steady in their manner.

- **AUTHORITIES** – An Authority will position themselves as the person with the best quality information, the one others rely on for advice and insight. So they will look to you like the **ANALYZER**. Their manner will often appear more withdrawn and tight.

In sum, these are the three primary distinctions to help you with Styles Identification. Over time you will presumably add or subtract from this starting point methodology, but this gives you a great starting point.

Unfortunately, sometimes you don't even have the luxury of a meeting before you need to make a deduction. In these instances, we want you to become better at reading signs— meaning you are really dialed in to whatever information you are getting back from the other person to make that first guess at their Style.

There are a few great places to really lean in and look for signals:

1. First Meetings

2. Written Communications

3. Approaches to Work

Let's look at each and go through the signals:

4. First Meetings

As you know, pressure is always the trigger for someone's Style coming out. That means a great place to start reading the signs is in first meetings when the pressure to make a good first impression is high.

There are four things to look for in first meetings:

5. 1. Behavior

Not an exact science, but generally you will notice:

- **CONTROLS** – A Control tends to move toward the head of the table, which is consistent with their Director positioning.

- **INFLUENCES** – An Influence is often the first one to introduce themselves to you and to make sure you get introduced to others, which is consistent with their facilitator positioning.

- **POWERS** – A Power tends to be distracted with other existing work waiting for the meeting to start or even come to the meeting late because they are so busy, which is consistent with their Builder positioning.

- **AUTHORITIES** – An Authority is often the one who is early to a meeting, reviewing all of the data, which is consistent with their Analyzer positioning.

6. **Work Space**

If you have the opportunity to meet with someone in their work environment, that is a great place to look for a reflection of what their Style is:

- **CONTROLS** – A Control tends to have a stylish and very clean office, signaling that they are more into dictating to others what they should do versus doing work themselves.

- **INFLUENCES** – An Influence tends to have an expressive and fun-looking work environment, often showing off pictures of friends and families as well as trinkets from different adventures taken in their lives.

- **POWERS** – A Power tends to have inclusive and busy work spaces, signaling that there is a lot of work going on in their environment.

- **AUTHORITIES** – An Authority tends to have a more functional and impersonal work space, signaling more of a serious work environment where things have to be done with precision.

7. **Time frame**

Pay special attention to the time frame in which the other person is relating to their business:

- **CONTROLS** – A Control has that 3-5 year into the future time frame, so they will often be focused on context, strategy, and vision setting for the business or their team.

- **INFLUENCES** – An Influence has a moment-to-moment time frame, so they may be speaking to you about issues happening today, and they will most often be issues about the personalities involved in the team or business.

- **POWERS** – A Power has a 90-day time frame, so their conversations will feel the most pragmatic about getting things done in the short run to show tangible results.

- **AUTHORITIES** – An Authority tends to focus first on the past, so they may start out by giving you the background on the team or the company before talking about current issues.

8. Body Language

Body language is a great tip for Styles Identification. Consider:

- **CONTROLS** – A Control tends to be pensive—serious and deep in thought about whether they feel you are competent.

- **INFLUENCES** – An Influence tends to be restless—wanting to jump from topic to topic, maybe even moving around physically.

- **POWERS** – A Power tends to be affable—wanting to make you feel comfortable so that you can get to work as a team.

- **AUTHORITIES** – An Authority will tend to appear a little bit more withdrawn—they might even have their arms crossed appearing skeptical about what you are saying.

At the end of the day, there is nothing magical about these four observations in behavior, but paying special attention to them will help you read the signs early on in a new relationship on your way to Styles Identification.

READING SIGNS IN WRITTEN COMMUNICATION

There are three primary areas to focus on to look for information about Styles in written communication:

9. Their Approach to Written Communication

Each Style communicates with a different approach:

- **CONTROLS** – A Control tends to be direct with their written communications—they don't beat around the bush and will often expect the same in return.

- **INFLUENCES** – An Influence can come across a bit scattered via written communications—as if they are telling you information in short bursts, and sometimes it may feel as though the information is not relevant to you.

- **POWERS** – A Power tends to be the most inclusive in their written communications—meaning they will often pull others into the discussion so that everyone is up to speed and on the same page.

- **AUTHORITIES** – An Authority tends to be the most detailed written communicators—they want to cover everything and make sure that they leave nothing out along the way.

FISHING FOR COMPETENCE VS SINCERITY THROUGH EMAIL

"My focus recently has been to try and figure out if people are sincerity or competence based through email communication. It's a little trickier than when people are talking because you can't pick up on the inflection of their voice.

Continued...

But I like the challenge of evaluating it based on nothing more than an initial email exchange.

"My practice is to put a little something in the beginning of an email that is personal and something I know about the other person, and then see how the other person responds to it. A recent example was I learned that a potential client had just spent a Sunday riding roller coasters with some of the other people that she worked with. So, I opened my email by briefly reintroducing myself, reminding her where she had met me, and then wrote something like, 'By the way, how were the roller coasters? Those things terrify me!', then followed with the info that I needed. When I got her response, she didn't reference the roller coasters at all, which told me that's she passed on the sincerity bait and went straight into competence. That's just a little indication about how to deal with her moving forward, making sure I'm crossing all my t's and dotting my i's with her and forgoing making a personal connection at the beginning, starting all of my emails with a business focus. I feel this allows me to make a better connection with people faster, and I just take it from their email communication. It's amazing what people tell you without knowing they're telling you. It's become a game to figure this out as quickly as I can!"

10. Look and Feel

From the length of a written response to the type of punctuation used, all of these things can give you clues about someone else's Style. Let's use an email example where you write someone and ask in the Subject line, "Are we on for tomorrow?"

- **CONTROLS** – A Control tends to be very short with their written responses, sometimes just one word or even one letter (like Y for yes, N for no).

- **INFLUENCES** – An Influence tends to also write shorter emails but will often include more sincerity-based language, emojis even, and they might include things that don't feel as relevant to your email.

- **POWERS** – A Power tends to summarize into action points since they tend to think in the form of an agenda. Also, they will often attach to do lists to help keep everyone on track. And finally, they will often include others in the process.

- **AUTHORITIES** – An Authority tends to write the longest communications, as reading is their desired medium for learning. So when you see follow-up notes, longer emails, and attachments, etc., it is likely they are from an Authority.

11. How You Describe Them

As you are receiving written communications from others, pay attention to the adjectives you are using in your mind to describe each:

- **CONTROLS** - For a Control, you may find you are using adjectives such as rational, determined, systematic, and smart.

- **INFLUENCES** - To describe an Influence, you may find that you are using adjectives such as adventurous, open, flexible, and fun.

- **POWERS** - For a Power, you may find you are using adjectives such as practical, dependable, hard-working, and steady.

- **AUTHORITIES** - For an Authority, you may find you are using adjectives such as organized, critical, intelligent, and rigorous.

Now that you have some ideas for how to identify the Style of other people, it is important that we set aside our own Style before we make that phone call, write that email, or go into a meeting.

This is what we mean by **Neutralize**, which is the topic of the next chapter.

CHAPTER 12

NEUTRALIZE

"Knowing yourself is the beginning of all wisdom."

— Unknown Author

A s difficult as it feels to identify Styles in others, it pales in comparison to how hard this next step truly is.

In order to M.I.N.E. for Diamond, step three requires us to set aside our own Style. Meaning that we need to neutralize our own Style.

The dictionary definition of neutralize is "to render (something) harmless by applying an opposite force or effect." Conceptually, this makes sense because in our thinking brains (our neocortex), we understand that applying the Diamond Rule means not focusing on ourselves.

But then our biology kicks in!

Once this happens, the drugs go to work and our body begins to take over our mind. This is why many times after a pressure-filled situation someone might say to you, "I can't believe you did that!" or "I can't believe you said that!" and you have no recollection. In that moment, your amygdala was running the show, and you only re-entered the picture after the pressure subsided.

In order to successfully neutralize your own Style, you have to initiate a process of witnessing yourself interact with others—in other words, become an observer of yourself. We know that sounds strange, but in the same way that sports players watch video of themselves so that they can learn ways to improve, we need to be able to run tape on our interactions with others. Doing this will enable us to notice what causes us to feel pressure in business and what our biology does when that pressure hits.

Only then can we apply an opposite force.

To that end, there is a four-step process to engage in for neutralizing your own Style:

1. Seeing your pressure triggers

2. Managing your biology

3. Clearing your Head

4. Making your Style disappear

Let's look at each in a bit more detail:

1. Seeing Your Pressure Triggers

When we go back to the basics, the game of business is a game for identity. This fundamental is critical because as you pay attention, you will begin to notice that there are certain things that happen in the game that cause you to feel as though your reputation is about to be damaged.

While certain things like not meeting a sales quota or losing our job would be a direct hit to our identity, many of the day-to-day events are not quite as extreme and some may not even be real.

Many times we react to situations biologically even though any risk to our identity is just a figment of our imagination.

We take things personally. We get angry at how someone is doing or not doing something, and we think their action or inaction is directed at us.

These moments we call "pressure triggers." The better we get at identifying them, the sooner we can intervene in the message the drugs in our brain are sending us and keep our neocortex engaged.

Typically, each Style has a certain primary pressure trigger:

- **CONTROLS** - When a Control takes their idea out to others, often times they expect full acceptance. When others begin to question or even negotiate a better way of doing something, if not careful, a Control may interpret this as someone questioning their idea, and they can take this personally.

- **INFLUENCES** - The primary pressure trigger for an Influence is often when they feel that they must dig in and do follow-through. These moments begin to look like a loss of freedom, which can have an Influence begin to feel impatient and upset, like someone is trying to fence them in.

- **POWERS** - The primary pressure trigger for a Power is often when they are starting to feel as though they are not being included by others. This exclusion can have them promise to take on more work, leading them to become overwhelmed with all that they have to do.

- **AUTHORITIES** - The primary pressure trigger for an Authority is often when they feel they might make a bad decision. This can cause an Authority to worry about their own competence, leading them to wanting to see more and more information, which can slow a project to a grinding halt.

A POWER SELF COACHING HERSELF OUT OF A BREAKDOWN

"After many years of working with Market Force, I feel I now have a fairly good understanding of where my weak spots are. As a Power, I know that when I get triggered,

Continued...

my instinct is to put my head down and tolerate the situation, just to get through it as quickly as I can. Most of the time I don't even speak up about things even if I disagree with what's happening around me.

"Now that I can see those things about myself, I work to coach myself out of that behavior. I tell myself, 'Don't tolerate, don't bottle it up, say something, don't avoid confrontation, you've got to overcome your biology and work yourself out of this breakdown even though it's tough.' I know my biology, so I give myself tasks to do. That's pretty hard for a Power to resist. Becoming more self-aware around my biology has been a huge part of my success over the past few years."

But while these are primary pressure triggers, it benefits each of us to dig deeper. So, by putting a little recorder on your own shoulder, you should start to pay attention to those things in your daily life that make you feel threatened and write them down for your awareness moving forward. For example:

- I feel pressure when I think someone is trying to take advantage of me.

- I feel threatened when I think someone is questioning my competence.

- I feel angry when I feel like I have no flexibility or options.

- It really bothers me when I feel like I am being ignored.

The more pressure triggers you can identify, the better. This is because when you hear yourself engaging in one of these internal conversations, you can begin the process of managing your biology.

2. Managing Your Biology

When we feel identity pressure, our body begins to go nuts. The reptilian brain lights up our limbic system, and our body begins to react. Learn to listen to your biology.

In order to manage your biology, then, you have to know what it does when the pressure hits. For example:

- Do you feel your heart rate increase?

- Does your breathing get shallow?

- Do you feel your hands begin to sweat?

- Does your face turn red and do you feel flushed?

- Do you feel adrenaline running through your body?

- Do you clench your jaw?

Whatever your biological reaction to pressure is, it's useful to begin to recognize when you have been triggered. This recognition gives you back *choice*. The choice is between treating business like it's life-or-death or maintaining perspective and using your neocortex.

AN AUTHORITY OVERCOMING CHALLENGES WITH INFLUENCES

"I have always struggled with Influences more than any of the other Styles. They are directly opposite of my Authority biology. We share none of the common traits by way of sincerity or competence, offense or defense. My instincts lean toward quality and precision, while they always focus on moving quickly, even if it means cutting corners. And, it just always seemed to me as if the world came so easily to Influences, which I'll admit made me resentful. Because of my Authority wiring, I just didn't understand or even respect Influences.

"But learning Market Force has helped me develop a true appreciation for the Influence Style. When I did the training it was like, 'Oh okay, I completely understand how they're wired now. I can see that they migrate on to something new because that's where they feel they can add the most value, not because they're flighty. They focus on relationships the way I get focused on quality and details. And I can see that they are responding instinctually, just like I am. That's just how they're wired.' This allowed me to see them without all the judgement I had been carrying and to appreciate Influences in a way I hadn't before. It was amazing. My struggle with them just began to vanish with this new understanding. In fact, the more I learned how to empathize with the Influence style, the more I truly began to appreciate the value they bring. This has served me well ever since."

To assist in the process, we offer the following three simple steps for managing your biology:

1. Breathe

Pressure can literally take your breath away. Remembering to breathe when you catch your biology going crazy will help you calm down and get re-grounded.

2. Focus

Go back to the basics and remind yourself that business is just a game, and that you are working to build a specific identity in that game. Reconnect with why that identity is important to you and focus on how to keep moving forward in the game from your neocortex.

3. Go Diamond

Do what you can in the moment to observe what is going on for the other person. There is a strong likelihood that if someone triggered you, they were triggered themselves. By going to the Diamond Rule right at this moment, you may be able to relieve pressure for the other person, which could substantially enhance your reputation.

To be clear, none of this section on managing your biology is easy! It's really hard to do in the moment. In order to go Diamond, as was just outlined here, step number three is critical to your process.

4. Clearing Your Head

With your body hopefully now under control, you need to turn to your mind—your neocortex—and make sure that you are ready to mine for Diamond.

This is another thing that is easy to say, but hard to do!

However, it gets easier when we focus on the one thing that can make a difference: being judgment-free.

By clearing your head of any judgments you have about the other person, the pressure, the situation, whatever, and attempting to work from a clean slate gives you the best chance to be on your game. In essence, the price of admission to effectively applying the Diamond Rule is that you are able to work from this type of clean slate. This means you are able to turn off your own Style, manage away the things that bother you, and not listen to your own internal conversations while you are interacting with others.

Depending on the severity of the situation, here are a few techniques:

1. *Low Pressure - Reconnect to Diamond*

   If you are feeling good biologically, then just reconnect quickly to the Diamond Rule before you engage with another person. Whether you take five minutes or just thirty seconds before you go into a meeting, join a teleconference, or return an email, take that bit of time to set aside your Style and your concerns so that you can truly listen to what is going on for others.

2. *Medium Pressure - Call a Time-Out*

   If you can tell you are triggered, look for a way to call a time-out. Maybe just excuse yourself to use the restroom in order to get out from underneath a tough conversation. Anything is better than going forward when you are biologically triggered. Learning to cool off a bit and clear your mind before you engage is a very good practice.

3. *High Pressure - Download Before You Go*

   If a situation really has you, it is a great idea to find someone to confide in, but preferably find someone outside of your own team. That person should be focused on helping you separate the facts of the situation from how you feel about the person and your own judgments. If you choose to download with someone on your team, understand the risk that you may unintentionally trigger that person as well, and then they won't be very useful in helping to calm you down.

Ultimately, steps 1 and 2 are for managing your body, while step 3 is for managing your mind. Together they give you opportunity to fully neutralize your Style, which is step 4.

4. Making Your Style Disappear

Styles is not an attempt to pigeonhole you or lock you into any particular way of being. In fact, the point of knowing your own Style and understanding your pressure triggers is the exact opposite. The point is to help you become more resourceful and achieve more in life. Your biology wants to keep you in a box, to keep you focused on saving your own life even though the game of business is not a life-or-death game.

BECOMING STYLE NEUTRAL THROUGH AWARENESS

"I remember several years ago, sitting in a meeting with someone and we were talking about Styles. He asked me what I thought his Style was, and I told him he seemed like an Influence to me. He was impressed with my observation and told me I got it right. Then I asked what he thought my Style was. He said he had no idea. He expressed that I seemed pretty balanced and had characteristics across the Styles. I thought that was the best

Continued...

compliment I've ever received, not to be so dominant in one Style that people could recognize it. Even though I know, of course, where I go in my stress and I know what points of pressure can get me, being so neutralized that others cannot recognize your Style is a great aspiration, at least in my opinion."

The way out is to make your Style disappear. Consider:

- Once you identify your pressure triggers, you are quicker to manage your biology.

- Once your biology is under control, you feel more balanced and more able to use your neocortex to work through whatever is in front of you.

- Once your neocortex is more engaged when pressure hits, you feel more focused.

- With balance and focus, you are able to zero in on doing what is necessary to move the relationship forward.

These outcomes allow you to look at the situation more objectively and not through the lens of your own Style. It's like taking off a pair of glasses you did not know you were wearing so that you can look onto whatever situation you are in with a clear view.

AN INFLUENCE ADJUSTING BEHAVIOR TO BETTER SUPPORT RELATIONSHIPS

"I'm an Influence and I think the biggest impact the Diamond Rule has had on me is that it's really helped me slow down when working with and selling to other Styles. All of my instincts are to move fast. I want everything to be done right now, even the deals I am working on with my clients. After learning Market Force, I now take a moment when I feel that instinct clicking in, because I realize that my natural pace can cause other people to get uncomfortable. Honestly, I realized I was putting a lot of my teammates and clients on edge without even knowing it. Understanding how my Style was impacting others has really helped my business in a profound way. Now I am taking care of others, which is actually one of my primary goals as an Influence."

This is where we take you back to the beginning of the book to remind you about the two different types of pressure we will face as human beings.

So one more time, let's use a diagram to distinguish what we are saying:

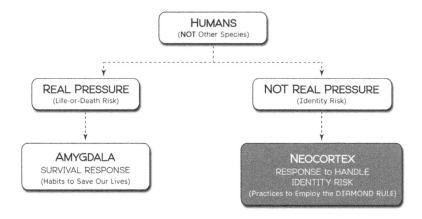

So, if you are ever in a life-or-death situation—trust your Style, your amygdala, and your instincts. They give you the best chance to live.

But when in the game of business, make it your goal to be someone whose Style others cannot figure out.

RESULTS YOU WILL EXPERIENCE FROM NEUTRALIZING YOUR STYLE

As you work on neutralizing your own Style, there are at least three benefits that come along as part of the package:

1. *You Become More Resilient*

   As you play the game of business with less of a life and death perspective, your resiliency under pressure grows. This enables you to take on more clients, deal with bigger issues for your clients, and become more valuable to your clients.

2. *You Gain Confidence*

   As you learn to better handle pressure, your confidence just inherently increases. You look at situations with a renewed focus on solving issues, not treating situations as if they are dire. Using your neocortex more and more will give you greater insight into how to deal with situations that other people cannot because they are freaking out.

A POWER PURPOSEFULLY LOOKING TO SELL TO CONTROLS

"All the characteristics of Power are completely consistent with how I act, who I am, and how I like 30-60-90-day plans. My greatest strength isn't coming up with new ideas, but man, I can implement the heck out of them. That's why I usually sell best to Controls. I go in, I listen for what they're trying to achieve, I think of their needs as my checklist, then I just be myself and things seem to work out really well for both of us."

3. You Stand Out

Because you don't feel pressure as quickly as those around you, you will begin to differentiate yourself from others in the game. Clients will appreciate your approach and will begin to move away from others who increase their pressure. They will like working with you because you are able to reduce their pressure.

AN INFLUENCE OVERCOMING A NEGATIVE REPUTATION

"I am an Influence through and through. When I started learning Market Force, I was going through a period in my life where I was generally saying yes to everything, from projects at work to asks from my clients in negotiation, everything. I was overcommitting and overcompensating for relationships everywhere, and I was never saying 'no.' But you can't go to every networking event, you can't give in on every business point. But I was trying, and what I was trying to do was have great relationships absolutely everywhere, which clearly is impossible. And, the worst part of saying 'yes' and then not coming through, was that I was beginning to be seen as flaky, which was damaging the very relationships I was trying to create. That was one of those existential moments that got me to start changing. My Market Force training brought this problem to the surface, and it also has given me the tools to change my behavior. For that, I'm so grateful. I tell people all the time that Market Force has allowed me to do things I simply could not before I learned the tools."

The previous chapters will prepare you to do the most important thing for your clients as it relates to mining for Diamonds. That's the ability to **Empathize**. Let's examine that now.

EMPATHIZE

"Empathy is seeing with the eyes of another, listening with the ears of another, and feeling with the heart of another."

– Alfred Adler

Once we apply the first three steps in our quest to M.I.N.E. for Diamond (namely Mindset, Identify, and Neutralize), we reach the moment of truth.

This moment is Step Four, and it is where we apply everything we have learned and Empathize with those around us under pressure as opposed to focusing on our own needs.

The dictionary definition of empathy[9] is "the ability to understand and share the feelings of another." Once again, conceptually this appears relatively easy to understand. The application of actually putting ourselves in the shoes of others, however, is the difference between understanding the Diamond Rule and actually building your business game around applying the Diamond Rule.

And this difference is the difference between good and great!

"When you show deep empathy toward others, their defensive energy goes down, and positive energy replaces it. That's when you can get more creative in solving problems."

— Stephen Covey

In order to empathize with other people, there is a requirement that we authentically view the world through the perspective and feelings of others, something that is impossible without the step of neutralizing our own Style. Said differently, you can only be in one pair of shoes at a time. The upside to your identity and your

9. https://www.lexico.com/en/definition/empathy

relationships, however, is game-changing for sales and sales leader-ship when you can make this shift.

A SALES TEAM LEADER GROWING RELATIONSHIPS USING THE DIAMOND RULE

"A good time to think about the Diamond Rule is when you are looking to accomplish something that requires the involvement of multiple people, which is something a salesperson or a leader is doing on a consistent basis.

"The first thing you need in business is to be liked and respected. You have to be able to successfully manage re-lationships with a wide group of people. That's the foun-dation of everything. I think friendliness comes down to a few things: being engaging, showing vulnerability, having positive intent, and being accountable. With these things it becomes relatively easy to bring a group together to work effectively. People will want to work with you, and you'll know who the right people are to work with. That's step one.

"The second step is taking that friendliness through to execution.

"In most instances where there is friction, such as where there may not be a common goal or someone may have priorities different than yours, the pressure gets elevated. The easy thing to do in those moments is to implement assertiveness as a tool, which may achieve the result, but it is not scalable, and it will definitely diminish your friendliness over time. Assertiveness is a limited re-source, and the more you use it, the less people will want to work with you.

Continued...

"This is where the value of the Diamond Rule makes all the difference. There are tools like empathy and trying to understand where others are coming from that require listening and asking the right questions. It means going deep to find something that is motivating for the other person, which then gives the other person a reason to want to work with you that was not already established. That's harder to do, especially when you are under pressure. You have to be more patient and you have to have energy to do it, but it's the more successful approach in the long run.

"I'll admit that it's hard to apply empathy, thinking clearly about the people around you and how you can communicate with them to further the mission and objectives. The more that you can manage yourself in your own biology and be more self-aware, the more you will be able to use empathy, and you'll have a better chance of getting to the right outcome and maintaining the trust you've built with others."

For the final element of the M.I.N.E. process, there are three things to focus on in order to help you Empathize with others:

- Relating to people as a set of concerns

- Helping others grow their identity

- Delivering on the relationship

Let's look at each in more detail:

1. Relating to People as a Set of Concerns

The amazing thing about empathy is that it gives us a way to think and feel about others that is unique. Part of the uniqueness is the ability to distinguish between seeing others as problems versus understanding that all of the Styles have certain biological concerns and those concerns get triggered in the game of business even though logically they don't need to.

A CONTROL GROWING IN EMPATHY

"I'm a Control and as a result of learning Market Force, I work on being very conscious of Styles these days. Practicing empathy is the biggest growth area for me. The biggest challenge is remembering to do it in the moment of pressure, because I can easily get caught up in my ideas, my strategy, what I think should happen. And, even when I do remember, I sometimes find it boring to slow down and focus on being conscious of others. But when I force myself to do it, to really seek to understand what's important to other people and to find out what they think and what they want, it gets so much easier because it's like they're giving me the answers to the test. I realize now how hard I can make things for myself and others. Empathy solves all that."

To understand this further, consider the dictionary definitions of "problem" and "concern."

- **Problem** - a matter or situation regarded as unwelcome or harmful and needing to be dealt with and overcome

- **Concern** - a matter of interest or importance to someone

When we think of people as problems, we begin to see everything through the lens of being "unwelcome or harmful" to us. This leads each of us to take things more personally than we need to and potentially to even start protecting ourselves from others in order to make sure we are not negatively impacted. Furthermore, we may begin to inject the actions of others with negative intent—"this person is doing this to me because they are a problem." There is almost zero chance of working together in a collaborative or constructive way when people are viewed as problems.

AN INFLUENCE OVERCOMING BIOLOGY TO USE THE DIAMOND RULE WITH AN AUTHORITY

"As an Influence salesperson, I'll admit that the financial part of a deal is not my strong suit. Because of this, I surround myself with teammates who are super strong in that area. I can specifically remember I had a new bookkeeper who emailed me one day with some financial statements, asking, 'Are these okay? Have you looked at the balance sheet? Have you checked the P&L?' Ordinarily I would have quickly responded with, 'No, that's your job,' but that day I stopped and thought to myself, 'Wait, she's an Authority. Is this how *she* would like to be treated?'

Continued...

I caught myself moving so fast that I almost missed the Diamond Rule. So, I got on the phone with her and we went over the financials step-by-step. I remember being fascinated by the idea that going through this level of detail would be exciting for someone, because after all, numbers are what they are, you can't change them. But for her, it really was exciting, I could just hear it in her voice and feel it in her energy. And because I'm easily influenced, I found myself getting interested in what she was excited about. So, I began asking her meaningful questions and digging deep. We probably spent an hour and a half on that set of financials. We went over everything. Truthfully, at the end of the meeting I had less energy, but I could tell she had more. So for me there was a moment of 'Aha! Maybe I should do this more often with her!' It's become a great way for me to build loyalty and trust with my teammate. Huh, maybe I need to start doing that with my Authority prospects!"

The alternative then is viewing other people as *a set of concerns.* What is "of interest" to them (not us!)? What is "important" to them (not us!)? When we come from this set of questions in our relationships with others, we automatically reduce pressure in the environment by removing the background of negativity. We begin to look at the world from different perspectives, not our own, and we are able to avoid any connection to infusing the action of others with negative intent. Most people in business are not trying to sabotage outcomes by doing things to harm us or to hold us back— instead they are dealing with pressure, having their bodies become triggered, and are not even realizing it.

When we are the person relieving their pressure, we become more successful.

Said succinctly, when we stop seeing people as problems and start seeing them as a set of concerns, we can empathize with others and become a solution to their concerns by relieving their pressure.

PURPOSEFULLY WORKING THROUGH A BREAKDOWN WITH A POWER

"My partner and I had an enormous deal in process with a Power prospect when a breakdown suddenly arose during the due diligence period. I'm a Control and my partner is an Authority. Our instinct was just to solve the issue at hand. We're competence-based, and we don't like it when things go wrong. It makes us look bad. However, the Diamond Rule taught us that in these moments with Powers, they are more interested in feeling like we are all working together to get through the problem. They want to know that you care about the breakdown and any impact it's having. They want to feel your concern. So, we overcame our instincts and chose instead to meet with her in person right away. She was concerned for sure, but she was very appreciative that we would go out of our way to work through our fixes with her in person. We took care of the problem, but more importantly, we were purposeful about maintaining our relationship in the process. This person has become a great ongoing client for us."

2. Helping Others Grow Their Identity

When we go back to the foundational claim that the game of business is a game for identity, we can absolutely empathize more with others by anticipating what they are worried about when pressure hits. Most people in the game of business are so worried about their own identity when there is adversity that no one takes a minute to think about those around them. Left to our biology, we will all focus on our own personal brand or reputation.

But what happens when we flip that perspective on its head? What if, when there is pressure, we focus less on our own identity and more on helping others with their identity? Since that is the purpose of the game, we know everyone is worried about their own identity, so what if we focus outward instead of inward?

This approach changes everything.

A POWER WORKING WITH AN AUTHORITY TO GET THE SALES PREP DONE

"I'm a Power and I was working with an Authority on a big presentation. We spent four days working on the slide deck, which to my Style is way too much time to be spending on a slide deck. But I would present it and then we would talk about it and then my partner would have five pages of notes for us to go through. Then we would revise, and then there were four pages of notes and then there were three pages. You get the point! There were just always notes and more information. I was doing my best

Continued...

to be patient and working to meet my partner where she was and address her concerns since it was our presentation and our respective identities at stake. Finally, it got to the point when I was like, "Look, we have to do this, we have to call it and go meet with our client." She was okay with that after I listened to her concerns throughout the process. I don't think I would have gotten through that situation without the Diamond Rule—we would have fought every step of the way. And that's what is so interesting to me now, I mean I see Styles everywhere."

We know that the game of business is not a survival game—we have established that even if we fail in business, we don't die. And we know that the most successful people in the game are great at creating, establishing, growing, and managing their identity over time. Those are the ones who win more often in the game. What happens when we become the person that focuses on helping everyone around us win the game?

The answer is that we build such great relationships with those around us that we are consistently relied upon by others in their time of need.

AN AUTHORITY LEARNING TO OFFER MORE VALUE TO A CONTROL BOSS

"When I work with my Control boss, he gives me lots of projects with research and information he wants done. I realize he's going to give me lots of them because he's

Continued...

got many ideas and things that he wants to explore. As an Authority, I don't push back on him with cautions about the projects, at least not too early in the process. It actually helps him make more convicted decisions about what to pursue and what not to pursue when he just takes the research I do for him and then decides what he wants to do with that information. It helps him determine if he wants to push certain ideas forward or not. Essentially, I use the Diamond Rule to try and not get bogged down by the negative components I might have about his new ideas, which as an Authority is easy for me to do if I'm not careful. In short, I've learned over time that by applying Market Force principles to my relationships, I am respecting people more. It's been an interesting and more effective way to do things."

If you are looking for a reason to assist others with their identity, and a definitive reason to empathize with others, consider this: business is the only true win-win game on the planet.

Every other game people have invented (from poker to baseball, board games to soccer, chess to tennis, etc.) is a win-lose game. There has to be one person or team with more than the other. There has to be a victor and a conquered.

Business is actually a reciprocal game—the more we help others with their identity, the more they will help us with ours. It is a true win-win game. In sales, the more we understand and empathize with our clients and think less about our own identities and bank accounts, the more we can assist others in getting what they want from the game.

The more we do this, the more others want to assist us in getting what we want—either through giving us more transactions to work on or making referrals for us so that we can get more new clients.

AN INFLUENCE USING THE DIAMOND RULE TO LEVERAGE TEAM STRENGTH

"As an Influence, I usually lead the sales presentations for my team as I'm the most relational one of the three of us, and I connect well with people. I have a couple of Authorities on my team and while I like to have them at sales meetings to answer more technical questions that may come up, I don't like to have them presenting, as they can lose the room. Authorities are very interested in the data even when the client is not. And, truthfully, neither is very comfortable presenting anyway. They'd rather just respond to questions as they come up.

"But with a recent client opportunity (that didn't go great), one of my guys pointed out after our first meeting that it seemed liked the prospect was an Authority like him. His analysis of the interactions was spot on, and he showed me where I missed some key moments to provide more depth. Once he pointed that out, it was totally obvious to me, and I realized that I was actually the one losing the room in that meeting.

"To support his point, he had prepared some additional slides to add to the deck to better appeal to the needs of the prospect. To be honest, they were slides that I would never have presented, because in my mind, there was way too much information, and they looked boring. But I trust-

Continued...

ed his instinct and asked him if he would present them. He got very nervous about it because he's gotten a lot of dead stares and drool on the table in the past. But I reminded him about the Diamond Rule and helped him see that he would be the right person to present to this prospect.

"To help him feel more comfortable, I helped him practice leading from the front and tried to ask meaningful questions to help him feel prepared and build his confidence and cadence. In the end, he did a great job and really impressed the prospect in a way that I never could have. I was really proud that my teammate had the right instinct and overcame his defensive nature to play offense with me in front of the room.

"I really learned a valuable lesson—turn to others, ask those around me to make decisions, or ask them to lead the group, lead the charge. I think you can build a lot of emotional currency with others when you do that."

In the end, the game of business is a game for identity, but it is won on empathy. The more we empathize with others by helping them with their identity, the more others will help us in return.

MAKING EMPATHY ACTIONABLE

"Thinking about how you would teach empathy to others and how your would implement empathy with others are such powerful considerations. I think if you walked

Continued...

around in a company and asked people if they were being empathetic in their interactions with others, most people would probably say, 'Yes.' But my guess is that they are probably talking more about being courteous or kind or being easy to get along with more than they are really spending time walking in other people's shoes.

"Because of Market Force, my goal now is to encourage my salespeople to become a greater resource for the people they interact with, to recognize the desired identity each of their clients is looking to create and, in essence, become that resource to them. For me as a Power, this perspective has helped me play more of an offensive role as a leader to my sales team. I feel that it's kind of like going to the bowling alley with your kids and putting up the barrier so your kids can't throw a gutter ball. That's what the Diamond Rule has become for me. Literally every problem I've had or every problem that has confronted me or my team, I can now lay my biology aside and use the framework of the Diamond Rule to solve the issue. So far it hasn't failed me once. That's pretty incredible actually. My biggest experience with the Diamond Rule is that it has never let me down."

3. Deliver on the Relationship

Typically when we think of sales, we focus on what it takes to deliver a great commercial result for our clients. This is healthy and it is important.

But it's not enough to deliver according to the Diamond Rule.

If we are to truly empathize with those around us, we must not only deliver on the commercial requirements of a transaction, we must also deliver on the relationship. As Ben Stein says, "Personal relationships are the fertile soil from which all advancement, all success, all achievement in real life grows."

AN AUTHORITY DEEPENING RELATIONSHIPS WITH POWER CLIENTS

"The greatest value I've gotten from using the Diamond Rule is how it has helped me work more successfully with my Power clients. As an Authority, I use a number of tools with Powers to communicate better with them, always focusing on acknowledging their workload and the volume of the work they are getting done. I always make sure they know that I know how busy they are and how much I value their time and efforts. And it's amazing how my Power clients just glow when I'm able to do that. You can just see them literally light up. Once I do this, I always jump back into the priorities surrounding their projects so that they know I am a fellow hard worker. Truly, I feel way more connected to my Power clients thanks to the Diamond Rule."

The truth of the matter is that when we only focus on the commercial requirements with our clients, we tend to deliver only a lukewarm, energy neutral experience. In other words, "Meh."

Such a description is not enough for us to excel in the game of business. Consider all of the customer experience statistics that bring this to the foreground:

1. 67% of customers say their standard for a good experience is higher than it has ever been.[10]

2. 64% find their customer experience more important than price when purchasing something.[11]

3. 67% of customers say they will pay more for a great experience.[12]

4. 32% of customers will stop doing business with a person or a brand they love after only one bad experience.[13]

All of this data suggests that it is vitally important to deliver on more than the commercials in a transaction. Delivering on the relationship and reducing pressure for those around us is a great way to be seen as someone who delivers a great experience.

A POWER WORKING EFFECTIVELY WITH A CONTROL

"As a Power, I employ the Diamond Rule most successfully with a top client of mine who is a Control. We work together, hand-in-hand, on a pretty consistent basis. Because I've had my attention on what is and isn't im-

Continued...

10. https://www.salesforce.com/form/pdf/state-of-the-connected-customer-2nd-edition/

11. https://www.gartner.com/en/documents/2857722

12. https://www.salesforce.com/form/pdf/state-of-the-connected-customer-2nd-edition/

13. https://www.pwc.com/us/en/services/consulting/library/consumer-intelligence-series/future-of-customer-experience.html

portant to him, I've learned he definitely does not want super-detailed updates or too many specifics about what I'm working on for him. Instead, he appreciates high-level overviews, and he moves fast with just the basic details, always ready to make a decision and move on to the next thing. Now, sometimes he will dig in to details, but only when he wants to. Otherwise it's just about the big picture for him, because that is what calms his biology. So, the Diamond Rule has been huge for me in terms of relating to him and not triggering him unnecessarily, which has been important for our relationship. I just have to remember that he doesn't want things that a Power wants, so I stay curious about and focused on him, and it's worked out pretty great."

Richard Branson once said, "Complexity is your enemy. Any fool can make something complicated. It is hard to make something simple." This table shows a very simple way of thinking through delivering on the relationship:

SCENARIO	DELIVER ON COMMERCIALS	DELIVER ON RELATIONSHIP	EXPERIENCE
1	NO	NO	Energy Down
2	YES	NO	Energy Neutral
3	NO	YES	Energy Neutral
4	YES	YES	Energy Up

The idea is:

1. **Scenario 1**: If we don't deliver on the client's commercial requirements, and we don't follow the Diamond Rule and deliver on the relationship, the client will leave with an **energy down** experience.

2. **Scenario 2**: If we deliver on the client's commercial requirements, but we don't follow the Diamond Rule and deliver on the relationship, the client will leave with an **energy neutral** experience.

3. **Scenario 3**: If we don't deliver on the client's commercial requirements, but we follow the Diamond Rule and deliver on the relationship by caring for the client through the process, the client will at least leave with an **energy neutral** experience.

4. **Scenario 4**: If we deliver on the client's commercial requirements and we follow the Diamond Rule and deliver on the relationship, the client will leave with an **energy up** experience.

AN AUTHORITY OVERCOMING BIOLOGY TO WORK BETTER WITH A POWER

"I'm an Authority and one of the people on my sales team is a Power. One of the ways that his Style expresses itself is how he goes about getting things done. If the pressure's on and there's a choice between partially completing something in order to check it off his list or pausing long enough to make sure that it gets done right, he always seems to choose to the former. That just seems

Continued...

how he's wired, and this has been a constant friction be-tween us. He would always be ready to move onto the next thing, and I would always get in the way insisting that it had to be done exactly right. His argument was, 'If we don't get it done, if we don't meet the deadline, then the quality is not going to make much of a difference.' And we would have these loggerheads going a lot around this issue, and we struggled as a result.

"I wanted things to be different, so I used the Dia-mond Rule to help change our dynamic. I learned to be-come very selective about when I would insist on quality and when I would be okay letting things go. I realized that if I made everything important, then nothing would be. In fact, I started this self-reflective approach where I would challenge myself, 'Am I focused on quality here just because that's how I'm wired, or is this something that is really going to make a difference?' Just by asking myself that question, I learned to differentiate between those two things, which I had previously been blind to, and I was able to eliminate some of those points of con-tention between us. This approach has greatly improved our working relationship and helped him begin to under-stand what is really important and what isn't. This change has allowed both of us to focus more on making money than on dealing with each other, and we're both happier as a result."

The overall point of the table above is where we put our mindset. Most people in business aim for Scenario Two and believe that if they just deliver on the commercial requirements, they should excel in the game. However, this does not prove to be the case. By leaning in and empathizing with our clients, we give ourselves the best chance to thrive in sales. Therefore, engineering our mindset toward Scenario Four is the way to play according to the Diamond Rule.

The next step is to begin wiring ourselves for prosperity. Specifically, how do we leverage the Diamond Rule to win in sales and the game of business?

WIRING FOR
PROSPERITY
(THE HOW)

CHAPTER 14

BIG PICTURE

*"To be a champion, I think you have to see the big
picture. It's not about winning and losing; it's about
every day hard work and about thriving
on a challenge."*

— Summer Sanders

Winning in the game of sales means thinking at every step of the way about how you can apply the Diamond Rule and adjust your behavior to relieve pressure for those prospects and clients around you.

If we look at the life cycle of "selling to" and "working with" others, we can simplify things by breaking down the sales life cycle into six primary actions:

1. Reminding yourself of the other person's perspective before you meet with them—*setting the foundation* for success

2. Thinking about how you can make a *great first impression* on the other person when you factor in their Style

3. Coming up with effective ways for *working the sale*, including tips on handling negotiations and creating a win-win closing for your potential clients

4. Considering how you can better *manage the relationship post-closing*, including what to do if a breakdown occurs

5. Examining ways to *acknowledge success* once you deliver on what was promised

6. Focusing on things you can do to solidify your relationship with the other person after your work with them is complete in order to *set up for the next go-around*

Within each of these actions, there is a series of steps to take and areas to focus on that will help you create the best relationship and greatest identity possible with each of the Styles.

We will examine each of these in the following chapters, starting with "Setting the Foundation."

CHAPTER 15

SETTING THE FOUNDATION

"It is not the beauty of a building you should look at;
it's the construction of the foundation that will stand the
test of time."

—David Allan Coe

If you are going to apply the Diamond Rule when working with another Style, you must consider the other person's perspective BEFORE you meet with them. We call this "setting the foundation for success."

There are three primary aspects of setting the foundation for success:

1. Recognize their primary trust concern

2. Avoid pressure triggers

3. Know their primary business concerns

Let's begin by looking at the importance of sincerity and competence. Remember, over 80 percent of our judgments about others come down to these two factors. Knowing which one is most important. Let's examine the primary trust concern for each of the Styles.

1. Recognize Their Primary Trust Concern

In Chapter 8, we demonstrated that while all people consider the same elements when they are building trust with others, they consider those elements in different orders—so a one-size approach does not fit all. In order to trust someone, we all need to believe that person to be both competent (skilled and capable) and sincere (honest and reliable). But, based on our biological wiring, we will evaluate only one of those characteristics at a time and won't assess the worthiness of the other until we are fully satisfied with the first.

So, when seeking to establish a foundation of trust with someone, it is essential to get a sense of which trust concern—competence or sincerity—they consider first so you can employ the Diamond Rule, managing your own biology and making their needs more important than your own.

COMPETENCE

The two Styles that tend to hold a primary trust concern for competence are Controls and Authorities. When interacting with either of these Styles, remember to keep the social or small talk to a minimum and be willing to move quickly into business-related discussions.

For Controls specifically, allow them to dictate the course of your meetings (as best you can) and be ready to **be direct and to the point** as that is the communication style they appreciate.

Authorities will be most interested in evaluating your background and your credentials to determine your competence. So, **be prepared with your evidence of past performance**. You may want to consider sending information beforehand when you meet with an Authority, then show up to the meeting and ask if they have any questions about what you sent over—it's a great icebreaker with Authorities.

SINCERITY

The two Styles that tend to hold a primary trust concern for sincerity are Influences and Powers.

Never forget that an Influence has a primary trust concern for sincerity and will want to get to know you before getting down to business. Therefore, when you are meeting with them, just relax if they want to take the first few minutes (or more) to discuss things that feel **more personal in nature**. You may even want to suggest the meeting take place somewhere that feels more relationship-oriented and personal—like a restaurant or a coffee shop.

INSIGHT INTO USING THE DIAMOND RULE TO BUILD GREAT RELATIONSHIPS

"I find that deep relationships are actually very hard to create because very few people are willing to listen and engage with curiosity and with a deep and genuine compassion for others. And that's exactly what the Diamond Rule calls for all of us to do. The Diamond Rule encourages us to be better under pressure, to think, 'I'm so curious about who you are and what's important to you that I'm willing to put my needs aside, engage with you, and be patient and be present with you.' Playing the game of business inside this great context of building deep relationships is where all my sales opportunities happen."

Similar to Influences, Powers have a primary trust concern for sincerity. However, unlike Influences, Powers only need a short period of time to know whether they feel comfortable with your sincerity. Go in prepared to demonstrate that you can connect with a Power, but don't overdo it with small talk because Powers want to see that **you are sincerely interested in getting to work** sooner rather than later.

A POWER LEVERAGING STRENGTHS IN THE SALES PROCESS

"The biggest value I've gained from Market Force is understanding the workings of my own biology. I've come to really appreciate my natural skills and strengths in a way that I just didn't see before. In particular I can now see that what I bring to the table is really valuable to the sales process. As a Power, I know that I've always been good at getting things done, but I'm also really good at bringing a deal together and holding it together, getting all the right people involved. Through this lens, I have found better focus on adding value to my sales team and to my clients."

2. Avoid Their Pressure Triggers

Now that you're off to a great start in your new relationship, having established a strong foundation of trust by noticing their order preference and sticking with that approach until you noticed their concern shift from either competence to sincerity or the other direction, your new goal is to maintain that level of connection. One of the things that can get in the way of that is unintentionally upsetting them with your words or actions. Things that can seem perfectly normal to you can easily ruffle other people's feathers.

CONTROLS

You will remember that a Control is primarily concerned about already knowing. Their Survival Conversation is: "I might die if others know I don't know." Once you are in front of them, avoid bringing up issues you know they don't have information about, and if you don't like one of their ideas, **be careful not to argue directly against them.** Instead, use the approach of asking logical questions so that they come to their own conclusions.

INFLUENCES

An Influence is concerned about their freedom, and their Survival Conversation is: "I might die if I have to do what others say." Therefore, when you are meeting with them, be sure to **avoid ultimatums at all costs.** Instead, look to show how your approach will be flexible if there is a need for changes and how you intend to keep the relationship at the top of the priority list throughout your process of working with them.

POWERS

A Power is concerned primarily with stability and inclusion, and their Survival Conversation is: "I might die if I am not included." When you meet with them, avoid conversations about moving so quickly as to destabilize the existing work environment. Be prepared to show a Power how **you have thought through a structure that should minimize risk along the way.** Be sure to work off of a task list, something Powers do often. Doing this will show that you have the pragmatic mentality a Power is looking for.

AUTHORITIES

An Authority is primarily concerned about security, and their Survival Conversation is: "I might die if I have to make a decision without all of the information under the sun." Based on this, when you meet with them, avoid moving too quickly or asking for too many decisions along the way. Instead, **take your time and walk through all options, then provide your recommendations** to attempt to relieve their decision-making pressure. Being a bit more methodical in your approach will go a long way with Authorities.

3. Know Their Primary Business Concerns

You're doing great, you've established trust and created great rapport with your new prospect. Now, when you are able to focus your attention on the things that matter most to each Style and prioritize those concerns, you will continue to build your valuable identity with them.

CONTROLS

A Control is often most concerned in business with two things: their image and being right. Keeping this in mind when you meet with them means looking for ways to **tie-in your ideas to their larger strategy** and attempting to give them credit for the genesis of an idea where you can. Obviously, don't placate or pander to them, but you should relieve their pressure with the tie-in strategy so that the starting point of an idea came from them.

INFLUENCES

Instinctually, an Influence is primarily concerned in business with their time and the relationships around them. Keeping these concerns in mind, work to **avoid slowing down the process** if you can and give options to choose from along the way. Be sure to talk about how your approach or ideas will incorporate the best interests of anyone involved in the project and how you won't sacrifice people in order to accomplish the goal.

A POWER FINE-TUNING THE SINCERITY APPROACH TO WORK BETTER WITH INFLUENCE CLIENTS

"I'm a Power and when I learned through Market Force that my Style shares a primary trust concern for sincerity with Influences, it didn't really make sense to me because I've always had a difficult time getting my relationships off to a good start with Influences. So, when I learned that their sincerity need is actually different than mine, it started to click. It turns out that we both need sincerity, but as a Power, I just need to believe you're a good person, that we share a strong work ethic, and you like to play fair. Once I know those things about you, I'm good and am ready to get down to work, because you know I love my checklists!

"But it turns out that Influences aren't looking for those same things. They're looking for a real connection as you would if you were making friends, not becoming work colleagues. Once I learned that, I realized that I've been turning them off all these years when I thought I was doing the opposite!

"Now one of my main strategies when I first meet with an Influence is to bring a ton of curiosity to the table. I go in completely present to their need to have sincerity, for their need to feel a sense of relationship and likeability, and I allow them to share all of their exciting ideas with me. I allow them to dream and then I ask a bunch of questions that show I care about them and also to help pull that dream out further. If I can let them know that I can help turn those dreams into reality, then I know I'm getting somewhere with them. Then, and only then, do I feel comfortable initiating any type of sales process. And, let me tell you, this approach works great!"

POWERS

Typically, a Power is primarily concerned in business with change and inclusion. It is important to remember that Powers are very collaborative by nature, and they value loyalty almost above all else (including competence). They like to **focus on 90-day intervals** to avoid instability and so that they are clear what's happening first, second, and third. In short, keep things simple and straightforward—a Power will appreciate it.

AUTHORITIES

Typically, an Authority is primarily concerned in business with the cost of products/services and driving efficiencies. Due to this primary security concern, many times the cost/benefit analysis is their go-to move to determine if something is worth the risk. To that end, make sure you **focus on the quality of your product or service** to attempt to have them weigh the quality against the cost. Don't be evasive when talking about the numbers. Be direct when answering such questions and be confident.

Now, let's look at creating a strong first impression with each of the four behavioral Styles.

CHAPTER 16

FIRST IMPRESSIONS

"First impressions matter. Experts say we size up new people in somewhere between 30 seconds and two minutes."

—Elliott Abrams

198 • DIAMOND GOLDFISH

Famous American actor Will Rogers once said, "You never get a second chance to make a good first impression." First impressions tend to be judgmental and shallow, and they actually have more to do with ourselves - our beliefs and our past experiences - than the person we are evaluating. Even with that bias, they wind up being accurate almost all of the time because of how our brains and psychology work.

When a first impression is made, it is immediately stored into our memory banks as "true," even though it is often based more on past interactions with other people in similar situations than on what we are currently experiencing. But, once we convince ourselves that the impression is accurate, our brains go about the business of amassing evidence to prove we are correct. This confirmation bias tends to ignore any evidence to the contrary. It reinforces the accuracy of our initial assessment, turning it from merely *an opinion* into *a fact* in our minds.

So, when meeting someone for the first time, one of the most important things you can do is make the best possible first impression. And of course, what makes for a good impression varies tremendously based on which Style you are interacting with.

Once you know the other person's Style, there are four actions you can focus on:

1. What to send beforehand

2. How to get each style talking

3. How to build credibility in a conversation

4. How to apply yourself to each Style's primary blind spot

We'll take a closer look at each of the four:

1. Before the Meeting

Often, the first impression you make with someone is the impression you make before you even meet with them for the first time. Once you've landed your first meeting with your prospect, here are the questions:

- What do you send them in advance?

- How much is too much and how little is too little?

- Do you send them anything at all?

Determining the right approach can be overwhelming until you remember Styles and apply the Diamond Rule. Let's look at how to handle each effectively:

CONTROLS

If you know you're going to be meeting with a Control, send them **an executive summary** in advance. They don't need much detail, just some high-level objectives and requests for their involvement, letting them know what to expect without making them do a lot of pre-work. Since a Control's *Greatest Fear* is being caught flat-footed—not knowing something they should know—they absolutely do not want to walk into a meeting unclear about what's going on or what's expected of them. If that happens, they will either skip out on the meeting entirely or come in aggressively asking questions like, "Why am I here?" or "What is this about?" You don't want them attacking your competence, which will definitely start things off on the wrong foot.

INFLUENCES

If you know you will be meeting with an Influence, all you have to send them in advance is **a relationship-oriented reminder**. Influences require the least amount of preliminary information before a meeting. However, because Influences tend to move quickly, sometimes they forget about upcoming meetings. To this point, you do want to be careful. Sending a reminder like, "Don't forget our meeting on Friday" or a calendar invite can feel like you are telling them what to do. Instead, make it a relationship-oriented reminder something like: "I am looking forward to seeing you on Friday!" This approach speaks to an Influence's focus on the relationship over the work itself.

POWERS

Send an agenda to a Power. Powers like to receive an agenda or an action plan before a meeting. They may not look at it before the meeting, although they will have it printed and be ready to go for the meeting itself. This is because Powers tend to take on a lot of work and will often be too busy to read anything before a meeting. You should still send an agenda because Powers appreciate that there will be a structure at the meeting so that they don't waste time. They also like to check things off of a list after they are discussed.

POWERS LOVE AGENDAS

"I recently had a big sales presentation in Dallas with a team I had never met. Since I'm a Control, I got there early, set up the room how I liked it, and then placed a one-page agenda on the table in front of each chair for

Continued...

the team that I would be meeting with. This is definitely a Diamond Goldfish practice for me, because as a Control, I don't need printed meeting agendas, but I've learned that they are important to other Styles, in particular Powers. So, that's why I do it.

"As the three people on the team filed in, I noticed how each person interacted with those pieces of paper. One sat down and just pushed it aside, probably a Control like me. Another one picked it up and thoroughly read it from top to bottom, taking in every piece of information, probably an Authority.

"Then a woman sat down in her chair, looked at the agenda somewhat incredulously, looking side-to-side as if to make sure this was really happening. She then returned to her agenda and sunk deeper in her chair with what appeared to be great satisfaction. A great smile broke across her face. She looked up and caught my eye then sincerely thanked me for providing an agenda for the meeting. She told me how important it is to her and that salespeople rarely provide this for initial meetings. At that point, I figured she must be a Power. So, I told her that I always put out agendas because about 25 percent of the people in the room want one (meaning Powers). This confused her and she asked me why I would bother if only 25 percent of people wanted one. I responded, 'Because 100 percent of the people in your chair want one.' That actually made her laugh out loud! It was a great icebreaker for the meeting."

AUTHORITIES

Send as much as possible to an Authority. Make no mistake, Authorities are the ones who want to see information about the subject matter of a meeting beforehand. Their primary trust concern is competence, so showing up without knowledge about the meeting makes them feel incompetent. When you add the fact that Authorities have the Hibernate Survival Strategy, it should be clear that they like to analyze as much as they can before having a conversation. On the other hand, if you don't send information prior to a meeting and you expect an Authority to make a decision, chances are they will say, "Let me review this information, and then we can meet again next week." In this case, you might have lost a week!

A POWER ADJUSTING THE SALES APPROACH TO APPEAL TO AN AUTHORITY

"As a Power, I would love it if everyone were Powers like me. Life would be so much easier! I get along great with other Powers because we speak the same language, we get each other, and we just love to get things done. They make so much sense to me and selling to Powers is a no-brainer. All I have to do to work successfully with them is just follow the Golden Rule. I just treat them how I would want to be treated. They love it, and it all works out great!

"But learning the Diamond Rule taught me that using the same approach for everybody is causing me to miss out on potentially 75 percent of the market. And as a Power, I hate to miss out on things! So, I've been building up my ability to treat others how "they" want to be

Continued...

treated, even when I'm feeling pressure and more than anything want to revert to the Golden Rule. This comes up a lot for me with Authorities because the way they think confuses me. The Diamond Rule showed me that when I'm not paying attention, I can potentially create conflict with Authorities if I push them too quickly into pulling the trigger. Since I am in technology sales, there are usually a lot of Authorities on the other side of the deal. So, I've had to get good at this.

"I recently had a sales opportunity with a Chief Technology Officer (CTO) that wound up going really well. This guy has a ton of responsibilities, and he is definitely an Authority. Using the Diamond Rule, I recognized the language he wanted to use with me and understood how he wanted to make a buying decision. Of course, there are similarities between our Styles—we are both more defensive than offensive, for example—but *how we make decisions* is very different. As an Authority, he was really focused on what happened in the past and needed a tremendous amount of information to feel good about making a future-oriented decision. Knowing that, I made sure to send him things in advance of our conversations, and every time I presented something to him, I made sure to give him everything he might need. I would then go away for a while so he had time to process, and when we'd come back together, he'd be ready to take the next step. This process is not natural to me, and I have to fight my feelings of frustration for how long it takes. But by understanding myself and the Style of this individual, I have been able to limit our conflicts and maximize our relations."

2. How to Get Your Prospect Talking

In sales, the more talking you do, the less identity you build and the less you learn about what's important to your prospect. The goal, as early as possible in a sales conversation, is to get your prospect talking. People's favorite subject is themselves, so as soon as you get them going, things start going your way. But how do you get them to begin sharing things of importance with you?

First, you have to ask "open-ended" questions, not "closed-ended" ones. The difference between the two is that you can answer a "closed-ended" question with a one-word response, like *yes* or *no*, or even *good* or *bad*. "Closed-ended" questions get you nowhere other than a verbal game of tennis, volleying short communications back and forth.

An "open-ended" question, on the other hand, causes people to think and forces them to provide you with a considered response.

For example, when your kid walks in the door from school and you ask how their day went, you may typically get that frustrating, automatic response of "fine," with no pressure to say any more, leaving you dissatisfied, wanting more. Most parents have learned to engage their children in more creative ways like, "Tell me about your day..." in order to get them talking. The same approach applies to your prospects.

Asking "open-ended" questions is clearly a good practice, but as we've learned, there are specific subjects and questions that strike more of a chord with the different Styles. Let's apply the Diamond Rule so you can ask them the questions that appeal to the way that they already think.

CONTROLS

Get a Control talking about **their big picture**. As we know, Controls have a biological **Dictate** Survival Strategy, which means that in first meetings Controls will tend to want to talk more than listen. With their focus being on the 3- to 5-year future, they mostly will want to share with you their vision for the future and strategic ideas that they have. Knowing this, it is never a bad idea to ask a Control person about their big-picture perspective to start off a meeting. The more you know about their vision, the more you can align your objectives with theirs, which is huge when working with a Control.

LET THE CONTROL PROSPECT DO ALL THE TALKING IN A SALES MEETING

"The Diamond Rule has become an instrumental part of my game. To me, it's all about adapting my approach to the Styles sitting across the table in moments of truth! Just today I was in a sales meeting where I instantly identified that one of my prospects was a Control and the other one was an Authority. It was obvious the second I sat down. The Authority person had our entire presentation in front of him, marked up with stickers and notes, and almost instinctively I began throwing detailed questions at him. The Control person, on the other hand, was leaning back, asking questions, telling stories, and dictating the flow of the conversation. I was just letting her speak, letting her tell us what we should and shouldn't be doing. The more I did this, the more engaged she got. I saw my role as repeating their language back to them, but in different ways. For the Control, I wanted her to know I understood her ideas, and for the Authority, I needed to show I was paying attention to the details. We scheduled an hour-long meeting, but because I just let the Control

Continued...

speak, the conversation went on for an hour and 45 minutes, and 75 percent of the time, the Control person was talking. My goal is to use a lot of the Diamond Rule tools in a very natural way. It has to feel authentic. It's amazing how well things proceed when you adapt the entire conversation to the Diamond Rule. When we left, they both said it was a fantastic meeting, specifically because I didn't come in telling them what they should do. And I'm a Control by the way!"

INFLUENCES

Get an Influence talking about **relationships**. Influences have a sincerity base to trust, and they are the most relationship-focused of all the Styles. Until they feel connected, it is difficult for them to move into a business conversation. Getting them engaged in more personal conversations is easy as long as you are sincerely interested in listening. Just asking them questions in an inauthentic way will offend an Influence (it's insincere!). Further, as you are asking them more personal questions, in return, be prepared for them to go through a similar line of questioning with you. When you get those questions, respond with openness, because Influences are looking for a connection and a professional relationship before transitioning to business.

POWERS

Get a Power talking about **their projects**. As we all know, Powers have a lot to do. If a meeting is going well, they will be sharing with you all that is on their plate. And, as you are learning about all of their to-dos, look for ways to have the Power feel as though you are coming alongside them and that you are willing to help them get things done. Due to a Power's sincerity base to trust, it is important that you demonstrate that you care about the projects the Power is working on and that you care about working hard yourself. Know that they can feel whether you are being authentic or not.

AUTHORITIES

Get an Authority talking about **the obstacles**. Authorities are strong analyzers of pesky details, including the details around where something could go wrong. Don't avoid the topic; go right at it and ask the Authority questions about where they see potential problems. When you do this, be sure to demonstrate that you are listening, maybe by taking notes and asking for more information. This will give an Authority comfort because they want to know they are being heard, that their assessments matter, and that you are someone who is looking to minimize the risk moving forward.

A CONTROL OVERCOMES NATURAL BIAS TO WORK EFFECTIVELY WITH AUTHORITIES

"I'll admit, it took me awhile, but I actually like working with Authorities these days. I'm a Control, and my problem was that I just didn't understand them very well and found them to be a lot of hard work. But now because of the Diamond Rule, I realize that they just represented to me the work that I actually didn't want to do in my own life. So, there was some real personal value for me in overcoming my bias against them. It allowed me to see their true value.

Continued...

"I have put in the time to learn how to work effectively with Authorities primarily because I wind up selling to quite a few of them in my line of work. The main thing I'm looking to achieve by following the Diamond Rule is help them feel less pressure. I think my old approach actually caused them to feel more pressure, not really a great sales technique! So, my new style is to slow down and listen and to provide way more detail than I would ordinarily otherwise. Certainly way more detail than I would ever need! And, since they typically want plenty of detail to analyze, I make sure to provide that to them in advance of every meeting and then give them extra time to make decisions. One other thing I do is try to schedule my meetings with them around 4:30 PM. I believe that Authorities actually think better at the end of the day because most of it is already all in the past. But, honestly, this also gives me the option of getting off the call by 5:00 PM, because they do like to talk a lot about all of those details, and sometimes I just can't make myself stay interested. Still working on that part."

3. Building Credibility in Conversation

You're off to a great start and you've just learned so much about your prospect by getting them to share what's most important to them. The next step is find the right approach to building credibility with them based on their Style.

CONTROLS

Due to a Control's primary trust concern of competence, you might think you need to discuss your credentials to demonstrate your competence to a Control. However, the application of the Diamond Rule that resonates with them is to understand their vision and then align your projects with their strategy for the future. In other words, put your resume away—that's for the Authorities! The credibility comes when you show a Control that you can **play the game of business at a high level** and contribute outcomes that move their vision of future forward.

HOW TO BUILD GOOD IDENTITY WITH A CONTROL

"Speaking on behalf of all Controls, what people could do for us is simply listen to what we have to say. When we speak, we've already put a great deal of thought into what we say and truly believe that we are offering you something of value. So, if you could just take the time to consider what we shared then reflect back to us your understanding of it, that would go a long way to helping us get less triggered. It matters so much to me if people can demonstrate that they have a fundamental understanding of what I'm talking about when I communicate with them. That is something that's really important to Controls."

INFLUENCES

Due to their primary trust concern of sincerity, it is important that you build credibility with an Influence by having an open and honest personal conversation until they are ready to move into a business conversation. And, due to their business concern for time, along with the fact that they move quickly, it is also important that you show that you are willing to work as quickly as they are. If you come across as impersonal or someone who will work too slowly,

Influences will be apprehensive about moving forward with you in a business capacity. Therefore, the credibility with an Influence comes through being **engaged and passionate** during the conversation.

AN INFLUENCE ADJUSTING TO THE NEEDS OF A CONTROL PROSPECT

"A few years ago we set up a dinner meeting with Mr. Big (a Control) in Chicago—no doubt a competence guy. This was a really big opportunity for our firm, and it had been really difficult just to get him to meet with us. He knows who he likes and he already knows who he wants to do business with. So, we used a fancy dinner to entice him, and he showed up with his team. When we met at the restaurant, we all shook hands and exchanged business cards. But when I handed mine to him, Mr. Big told me, 'I don't have a card on me.' It felt like such a Control thing to say.

"I let my team know in advance that we weren't going to lead with small talk, we weren't going to "get to know each other," we were going to stick to strictly business conversations. We were going to have to restrain our own need for sincerity to build trust with this guy. So, we sat and just talked competency with them for a while. We just talked. And, the whole time, the Control guy kept grilling us for competency, challenging our strategic thinking, posing difficult scenarios to see if we could follow, and we did a great job keeping our responses focused on what he needed, making sure he knew that we

Continued...

played at his level, and asking smart questions. Frankly, it was a bit exhausting for us, but we just followed the plan.

"Then, about two hours into the meal, he miraculously pulled out a business card from his jacket pocket and handed it to me with a slight grin and said, 'I don't give out my business card to people unless I'm sure they know what they're doing.' And that was the moment I knew we had just checked his competency box. It was such a relief because I'm not sure how much longer I could have kept that up. The rest of the meal was pure sincerity, and we all really enjoyed ourselves. And we still do business with that guy today.

"Before understanding the Diamond Rule, I would have just thought that this guy was all gruff and would have definitely missed out on this opportunity. This only happened because I didn't give him my Style (Influence) when we first met. I didn't give him anything sincerity-based, didn't try to build a relationship at first, just positioned my team's capabilities to perform on projects like his. He was just waiting for someone to tell him, 'We know what we're doing as it relates to your vision.' People with his Style aren't impressed by where I went to college or who I know in the city. They don't care where I grew up. They only care about how I can help them accomplish their goals in a competent way, at least in the initial stages. When you know what to look for, the signals are always there. Mr. Big sent very clear signals right from the start. He wasn't very smiley, not really interested in me or my background, and instead of getting triggered by that and making it about me, my team and I responded by just making it about him."

POWERS

It is important to factor in that a Power has a primary trust concern for sincerity, so it is critical that you build credibility with a Power by never coming across as rude or overbearing. Instead be seen as someone who will **be a hard worker and loyal throughout a project**. Powers do not need to talk for a long time about personal things to know whether they believe you are sincere, so you need to be ready to get to work as soon as they are ready to talk nuts and bolts.

AUTHORITIES

Combining an Authority's primary trust concern of competence with their time frame of the past means that it is important to provide Authorities with evidence of historical success. In other words, **your resume and credentials matter** most to Authorities! Early in the conversation, do not focus on small talk or even on making promises about what you will do going forward. Authorities will be more interested in the case studies of success on similar projects before they will want to discuss the next steps.

4. Positioning Your Value

While we know that each Style can certainly boast their own areas of strength, each can also struggle to perform in ways that other Styles do much more naturally. This becomes increasingly true when people find themselves under pressure.

As you work to build your identity early on with your prospects, knowing their Style gives you a huge advantage in the game, allowing you to more easily predict their greatest area of need—which provides you with the opportunity to position your value in a way that will be the most help to them. This area is what we refer to as their "blind spot."

A blind spot is something that sits outside of your normal field of vision. When you focus in one direction, it creates a blind spot in another. By definition, a blind spot is something you can't see, but it can be perfectly obvious to others around you. Think of it like this: When you are sitting in the driver's seat of your car, there are certain places hidden from your view. However, someone outside of your car can easily see what you're missing and can alert you if you are in danger. In that way, they would be really helpful to you.

Similarly, in business, if you can help people perform better in the areas "hidden from their view" that makes you a valuable partner to them.

The blind spots for the four behavioral Styles are:

- **Controls** have a blind spot where Influences perform most naturally—in the area of building relationships and showing empathy toward others.

- **Influences** have their blind spot where Powers perform most naturally—in building structures and having the discipline to follow through on promises they make to others.

- **Powers** have a blind spot where Authorities perform most naturally—in regularly reviewing their progress, knowing their priorities, and making sure all of the details get handled.

- **Authority's** have a blind spot where Controls perform most naturally—in confidently making decisions and having a strong conviction about their own ideas for the future.

Understanding these specific blind spots will allow you to position your value where each Style needs the most help. In doing so, you will build great identity with your prospects because not only will you relieve pressure for them but they won't have to admit to these things being an issue. You just handle the issue or concern before it ever comes up!

Let's look at how to do this for each Style.

CONTROLS

You would NEVER say to a Control in a first meeting something like: "I know you don't like people." Instead, you can offer to **help socialize their ideas with others** and rally others to their cause. That is something they don't tend to do naturally. Typically, a Control will feel less pressure when you offer to help them with spreading their good ideas around.

INFLUENCES

You would NEVER say to an Influence in a first meeting something like: "I know you struggle with follow-through." The better approach would be to look for ways to **describe how you will put in a structure** that will help the work to get completed and that will allow them to move on (or migrate) to new and more exciting opportunities. Doing this will help an Influence feel like you sincerely care about them.

AN AUTHORITY POSITIONING OWN VALUE INTO AN INFLUENCE'S BLIND SPOT

"I'm an Authority, and when I work with Influences in a sales situation, the most important thing I've learned to do is to help them with their blind spot, which is around the need for structure and their lack of commitment to genuine follow-through. I don't see these things as weaknesses in them, just areas they don't prioritize or pay

Continued...

much attention to. I use them to my advantage. I make sure that they know I'm really strong in the areas where they tend to struggle. Because of the Diamond Rule, I know these things about them even if they don't share them with me.

"Here's the talk track I remind myself of when selling to Influences. 'I hear all of your excitement and great ideas, and they're awesome! Now I need to position myself in your blind spot to be the person who can bring discipline and follow-through to your great ideas. I am the solution to your problems, and I can help you without taking away any of your freedom or your energy.' This is a fun thing for me. It's so great to be able to work proven strategies, and I feel like when I do this, I really am looking out for my Influence clients' best interests."

POWERS

You would NEVER say to a Power in a first meeting something like: "I know you struggle to find time to review the priorities and analyze what's working and not working." Rather offer to **track how we are doing against the project's priorities**—whether manually or through the use of technology—knowing that Powers like to know that someone is watching out for the overall success of the project. This allows them to keep their head down and focus on the work.

AUTHORITIES

You would NEVER say to an Authority in a first meeting something like: "I know you struggle with making decisions." Instead, you can look for ways to show how your processes will make the future more secure—such as how you have worked on similar projects or have experience in the area from the past. Your goal is to show how your perspective will **make future decision-making easier** to move through.

AN INFLUENCE'S STRATEGY FOR COVERING THE COMPETENCE SIDE OF THE TRUST EQUATION

"From my work with the Diamond Rule, the one thing I am absolutely committed to now is that if I'm going to a meeting with a new client, given that I'm an Influence, 100 percent of the time I'm going to have an Authority or a Control with me at that meeting. I want the Style on the other side of the table to be able to hear me or my team, and I've learned that people either have a primary concern for sincerity or for competence when they meet a new sales team. Because I am an Influence, sometimes I can be perceived as being disorganized or not serious. But if I have an Authority or Control sitting on my wing, I tend to get all the competence points my team needs. And you know, generally, I have not had any kind of an issue converting that prospect into a client. In most of our meetings, there are two of us there for a lot of different reasons anyway. But I would never put two Influence people in a meeting or two Power people or two Authority people. The Diamond Rule has taught me to bring complementary styles, particularly when there's a client interface going on, and we don't know who that person is just yet."

Now that we've set the foundation for success and made a great first impression, it's time to start working the sale.

CHAPTER 17

WORKING THE SALE

"Recognition happens when you see yourself from the inside out: as someone who can make an impact on the world instead of navigating the impact the world has on you."

—Justine Musk

Now that you have learned to hone your ability to foster strong first impressions with your sales prospects, your focus needs to shift to adding value to the sales process by treating them how they want to be treated as you further develop the relationship and opportunity.

In the course of managing the sales process, you must focus on optimizing your efforts in the following four areas:

1. Running effective meetings with each Style

2. Following up with each Style

3. Negotiating with each Style

4. Closing tactics with each Style

Let's tackle these in order, starting with making each meeting count.

1. Running Effective Meetings

As you would expect, the Diamond Rule tells us that different Styles appreciate different types of meetings, so here's how to best organize meetings for each of the four Styles:

CONTROLS

Due to the fact that a Control's primary trust concern is competence, they typically feel most comfortable meeting **in their office or in a conference room** in their office building. Meeting tone should be **short and direct**, and typically, it is useful to open by asking the Control to set the context and then, once they have, ask them what they would like you to cover first. These techniques give the Control a chance to dictate the direction of the conversation. Keep all answers **short and to the point** and only go into greater detail when they ask for more details.

INFLUENCES

An Influence tends to appreciate more **informal meeting environments** (such as coffee shops) due to their primary trust concern for sincerity. The meeting tone for Influence should be **engaging and casual** with the first bit centered on relationship-building and connection. **Allowing for tangents** empowers the Influence to feel that they can migrate through the conversation and that they have freedom in working with you. To help move the transaction forward, look for ways to support an Influence in order to turn their tangents into something tangible—but don't try to force them to be more structured.

POWERS

A Power typically is looking for you to be sincerely interested in getting a lot of work done. Therefore, they tend to like a **collaborative meeting environment where the focus is on the nuts and bolts** of getting the job done. The meeting tone for Power is **personal and productive**, meaning that you are working hard on their behalf to meet all of a project's deadlines. Avoid any pushy or aggressive behavior and **don't disrupt the process with conceptual conversations**. By keeping the meeting tactical in focus you will be appealing to a Power's concern for achieving tangible results.

AUTHORITIES

Because an Authority has a primary trust concern of competence, the best place for a meeting with an Authority is in **their office, in a conference room, or over the phone**. Authorities are less focused on the personal side of the equation and more focused on the data, so even a phone call will suffice. The tone of the meeting should **be precise and logical**, enabling the Authority to see the work that has gone into the presentation at every step. Avoid typos at all costs—Authorities will penalize quickly for such mistakes. Invite Authorities to ask questions and **be prepared with backup information** at every step in order to give them security in their process of working with you.

2. Following Up Afterward

Now that you've met with the prospect or client, you need to know how to best follow up with each of the four Styles:

CONTROLS

Due to a Control's focus on certainty, this Style absolutely hates surprises. With this in mind, it is important to **provide bullet point follow-ups** with Controls that remind them of the commitments both sides have made along the way. You can send along details for them to read if they choose, but the body of the communication should be short and to the point. Not doing the follow-up will have you looking incompetent to a Control, so it is imperative to make sure you do them in order to manage the relationship.

INFLUENCES

An Influence values freedom, so updates are a bit less important to this Style versus all of the other Styles. That said, **send visual updates (i.e., graphs, dashboards)** rather than written communication as that approach allows an Influence to quickly gauge where things are and move onto the next thing. It is important when working with an Influence to know that they typically are not detail-oriented, so you may need to plan on following up with them more often than the other Styles if you need information from them to move your sale forward. Make these follow-up requests via phone or in person instead of via written communication, because it keeps your relationship with them top of mind.

POWERS

Updates to a Power **should be regular and in the form of a checklist** with three categories: here is what we've done, here is what we are doing, and here is what we will do next. Powers have a concern for stability, so updates are typically very important to them. If a Power has not followed through on something, it is not because they have forgotten. Instead, it's usually because they have taken on too much. Therefore, if you are following up, do so with empathy and ask how you can help them move a task list item forward in order to stay connected with them on a sincerity level around trust.

AUTHORITIES

To an Authority, updates are critical. Given their primary concern for security, Authorities want and need the most information while working a sale. Therefore, your updates **should be consistent and detailed**—meaning that if an Authority has called you about an update, they are already upset. It is better to be overly communicative with an Authority during your process. Sending more details than you might otherwise think necessary is rarely a bad move. Even if they don't read everything, they will feel better knowing that you are on top of all of the particulars.

3. Negotiating Effectively

You've met and successfully followed up with your prospect or client. Now, let's up the ante and jump into how to negotiate effectively with each of the four behavioral Styles:

CONTROLS

Once you are in a negotiation with a Control, it's important to note that their approach to negotiation is **calculating**. They are like chess players looking for an advantage at every turn. Their primary concern in negotiation is for **their image,** in terms of how the final points of the deal look to others around them (peers, boss, etc.). The best approach with a Control is to **tie your proposal to their idea(s)**. Use language such as: "Based on your vision, here is what I think will make it work." This approach gives the Control ownership in your position during the negotiation.

INFLUENCES

Typically, an Influence has a less disciplined approach to negotiation than the other Styles, making it predictable that the process will be **unpredictable**. Influences are usually concerned for two main things: **time and the relationship**. They want you to move quickly and care for the relationship along the way. The best approach with an Influence is to **let them go first**—many times an Influence will give away more due to their concern for the relationship. Then, make sure you document commitments at every step, as Influences have a knack for forgetting previous conversations.

POWERS

A Power tends to be more **agreeable** in a negotiation than the other Styles due to their commitment to collaboration. However, **if they feel you push things too far, they will become obstinate** and difficult to negotiate with. A Power's primary concern in negotiation is for **structure,** as they want to know that everything can actually be completed on time and on target. The best approach with a Power is to create a **collaborative environment and then move toward a presumptive close** in order to show a commitment to action. Use language such as, "Here are the accountabilities on our side and here is all we need from you to get started. We are ready when you are."

AUTHORITIES

An Authority will tend to be **exacting and methodical** in negotiation and will likely want to do a deep dive into all of the details. Typically their primary concerns boil down to **cost and quality**—with cost being the very first thing they want to know before looking at anything else. The best approach with an Authority is to **be logical and have grounding** for each point of your negotiating position. Authorities are prudent and evidence-based. They will not respond well if your position appears irrational or if you appear too emotional.

EVEN A SEASONED INFLUENCE SALESPERSON CAN GET STRONGER BY FOLLOWING THE DIAMOND RULE

"One of my salespeople is a classic Influence who sells to everyone based on sincerity, a total relationship guy regardless of who he's selling to. Now, trust me, he does great, but like all of us, he has a pretty big blind spot in that area. The thing is that we work in the technology space and offer an enterprise solution with an average price point between $75,000 and $150,000. This means we often sell into Chief Financial Officers (CFOs) based on the function of our software. And, as you can imagine, most of them aren't very sincerity-based. So, sometimes my guy struggles with them.

"I had him participate in a Market Force training, and he was predictably gregarious throughout, jumping in all of the time, keeping everyone entertained. Well, they went through the analysis of Styles and he heard how Authorities often find themselves in roles like attorneys, engineers, accountants, and CFOs. It hit him that a CFO prospect he was currently working was more than likely an Authority and that he had probably been selling to

Continued...

him all wrong. At that point, he jumped into the conversation and with audible frustration in his voice, he said, 'So that's been the problem! It's so obvious now!' He realized that he had been starting with sincerity in all of his interactions with him, asking how he was doing, how his workouts were going, what vacations he had been on recently, etc. He then shared with the room, 'I know everything about this guy. I've done everything according to the standard sales script. I talk sports with him, I ask about his kids, everything, even took him out for a birthday drink. I think he loves me, but I just haven't been able to get him over the line.'

"When it was pointed out to him that he's not doing anything wrong, just working with this guy in the wrong order, he could now see that was doing everything right in the realm of sincerity, but that this prospect probably wants to focus on competence. And then a great moment of truth. My salesperson asked, 'Wait, what does that even mean? How am I supposed to focus on competence?' That was great!

"The response he got was, 'Well, it means talk about the business, talk about the project, find out what problems he needs solved. Talk details, talk specs. Share testimonials, talk about how you're solving problems for other clients.' His response was pure Influence, 'Well yeah, I do all that, but I wait until I establish the relationship.' And then you could see the light bulb go on in his head as he said it. He was approaching the prospect bass-ackwards, and he had never realized it.

Continued...

"At that point, it was as if he wanted to bolt from the workshop, as any Influence would, to go beat a path to his prospect's office. As soon as the training ended, he visited the prospect, determined to try this new competence-first approach. Without any chit chat, he jumped straight in with information, specs, and details, finally showing the prospect how much knowledge he actually had. And, to his great surprise, the prospect said 'yes' to the deal on the spot. It literally blew my guy's mind.

"Later that day, he sent this email to me and everyone who attended the workshop:

Subject: Accidental $80K Sale!!

Great presentation today, really enjoyed it. The Market Force program is remarkably insightful.

I made an unexpected $80K sale today as a result of using the approach shared with us this morning. I met with a long-term prospect who is terribly analytical, and I was able to address him in the meeting first on a competence level then through likeability. True story!

Would love for our team to do a follow up Market Force workshop if you all are interested. Otherwise, I will use my newfound skills to get our fearless leader to fetch us drinks at the next happy hour!

"I just think it's so important for us to remember that, even at the thinnest layer of the teaching of the Diamond

Continued...

Rule, we're relieving the misery that many people are experiencing. This Influence person was in complete misery from not being able to have his one-trick-pony way of building a relationship actually conquer his prospect. The prospect was in misery having to constantly answer questions about his kids and vacations without having his real concerns addressed. They were just talking past each other. It's really simple once you can see it, and just super frustrating without it."

4. Closing Tactics

From Alec Baldwin in the movie *Glengarry Glenross,* "ABC. A - Always, B - Be, C - Closing. Always be closing." To be effective in sales, you need to master how to close the sale. The author of this book's foreword, Anthony Iannarino, wrote an entire book on the topic.

So how do you best approach closing the sale across the four behavioral Styles? Let's find out!

CONTROLS

When working with a Control as a transaction moves to a close, it is important to **avoid an overemphasis on the details**. Typically a Control will want the details to be handed off to someone else, which you can anticipate by asking them if there is someone else you should handle this with. **Keep the conversation high-level and look to connect the closing with their original idea.** Controls move forward only when transactions fit their strategy and future orientation.

INFLUENCES

Moving toward a close with an Influence should mean that your **focus is on how the next steps after the closing will be fun**. By focusing on the relationship (i.e., "I cannot wait to work with you on this!"), you will be appealing to an Influence's sincerity base. Be careful to **avoid pushing them too much during the closing process** as Influences want to celebrate in a partnership-specific way, not feel like they are being manipulated. Make the actual transaction process easy since the details are not typically a concern for Influences. Instead, they will want to be focused on the next thing.

POWERS

In order to help reduce pressure for a Power during a closing, it's crucial to **avoid being unorganized with how the transaction process will unfold**. Almost nothing will perturb a Power more—because when they are ready to go, you need to be ready to go as well! You can move forward with a Power by **focusing on the specific next steps required, almost a presumptive close,** because Powers like working through a list and don't feel compelled to have the list be their idea. Keep the tone collaborative in nature, which is always a must with Powers.

AUTHORITIES

An Authority will be a bit more concerned about making a bad decision than the other Styles, so closing with an Authority can be tricky. You have to **avoid over-selling them,** because if you come across as too excited, they may begin to feel buyer's remorse and consider renegotiating the deal. Interestingly, **you need to be willing to walk away** from an Authority during a closing if they don't decide to move forward. Because Authorities are focused on security, if your walking away makes them feel insecure, that is often the best way to actually get them to opt in and sign on the bottom line.

A POWER SELLING WITH AUTHORITIES ON ALL SIDES

"After attending a Market Force seminar, I went to a business development lunch with my team. As I was sitting at the table, I realized that I was surrounded by Authorities. My whole team and every one of the clients were Authorities. This wouldn't have crossed my mind before. From the workshop I knew that if I did not flip into offense mode, we were not going to make a sale, just exchange a bunch of data and show each other how smart we were. So, I did my best to put on my Control and Influence hats and told myself not to be a Power. I'll be honest, I had to really pump myself up for this. I kept bringing the conversation back to what we were trying to achieve. I zeroed in on making sure everyone felt heard and their concerns were on the table. I kept the conversation future-oriented, incorporating all of the details and past evidence everyone had already shared to paint a picture of what the path forward could look like for them, providing the relevant details. I made sure to make recommendations that took the pressure off the Authorities to make a decision. It was a great outcome, and now I always look around when I go into a pitch and figure out which hat I need to put on to help move things forward."

Congrats! You've closed the sale and won the business! Your next step is learning how to manage the client relationship effectively—based on the four behavioral Styles, of course.

CHAPTER 18

MANAGING CLIENT RELATIONSHIPS

"Business happens over years and years. Value is measured in the total upside of a business relationship, not by how much you squeezed out in any one deal."

— Mark Cuban

Y ou've won the business—now you've got to manage it. The good news is that the Diamond Rule can be applied throughout the life cycle of delivering on the sale. Depending on the behavioral Style of your client, there are three actions you can take to help keep the relationship on track, even if there is a breakdown along the way. Here are three things you should be thinking about:

1. Staying connected to their focus

2. Avoiding their primary fear

3. Knowing what to do if a breakdown occurs

This is where you really want to stay on your toes. Often times in the sales cycle, this is where we can get a bit lazy, feeling like the deal is done. But Styles never sleep and we always need to be applying the Diamond Rule to truly be successful.

1. Staying Connected to Their Focus

You've done a great job so far identifying and speaking to the areas that are most important to your client. Now, here are some things to keep in mind as you continue your relationship with each of the four Styles:

CONTROLS

As we know, a Control is primarily concerned in business with their image. As you are working on a project with a Control, their unspoken concern will be: "Are you helping or hurting my image?" Keeping this in mind, consistently tying your ideas or changes back to their initial strategy is a great way to demonstrate that you are helping.

INFLUENCES

An Influence is primarily concerned in business with time and relationships. As you are working on a project with an Influence, their unspoken concern will be: "Do I feel connected to you and are you moving fast enough?" This means that checking in personally with an Influence and then demonstrating how you are working with energy and speed are critical to maintaining your relationship with them over time.

POWERS

A Power is laser-focused on production by nature. As you are working on a project with a Power, their unspoken concern will be: "Are you pulling your weight?" This means that along the way on a project, you need to make sure you are showing them how much work is being done, and you want to acknowledge their hard work as well.

AUTHORITIES

In business, an Authority primarily focuses on cost and efficiencies. As you are working on a project with an Authority, their unspoken concern will be: "Are you hitting your deadlines and the budget?" You will want to manage deadlines extremely well, and if you do miss one, apologize—and, due to an Authority's primary trust concern for competence, quickly turn your attention to providing details about what happened and how you are going to fix things moving forward.

USING THE DIAMOND RULE TO SWITCH HATS FOR DIFFERENT CLIENT NEEDS

"With my clients, very often we are dealing with two primary teams on their side, which map almost perfectly to Market Force Styles. They usually have a sales group

Continued...

> made up of Influences and an underwriting team of Authorities. I have to switch hats back and forth depending on the person I'm dealing with in the moment. When an underwriter calls with a question, I just dig into the numbers with them and don't worry about trying to build a relationship, because that's always a secondary concern for them. And in the next moment the phone might ring from someone on the sales side and I have to remember to be super relational with them, stop and take the time to genuinely connect with them before we start solving their business problems. Without the Diamond Rule understanding, this used to be crazy-making for me, and I had a hard time consistently giving my clients what they need. Now, it's just a system and the Market Force maps guide me perfectly. My life has gotten so much easier!"

2. Avoiding Their Primary Fear

The worst thing you can do at this point is trip over yourself by stepping into areas where your client feels most vulnerable. Your awareness of those pitfalls is important, so here are what they look like for each of the Styles:

CONTROLS

Avoid surprises. Not everyone likes surprises—especially in business. Controls hate them due to their Survival conversation of: "I might die if others know that I don't know." On the other hand, Controls do not want what they see as a ton of "unnecessary details." So as it relates to project updates, regular and concise would be the right amount. One of the biggest things to remember as it relates to

Controls is if you have bad news, share it right away—don't wait. If they find out from someone else, they may think you were keeping something from them, even if you were just trying to solve the issue before you brought it to their attention.

INFLUENCES

Manage the relationship. Of all the Styles, Influences tend to require the fewest progress updates and the least amount of information along the way. That is primarily due to the Migrate Survival Strategy and their desire to feel free to move on to other things. All of that said, Influences do appreciate a more personal touch—so instead of an email or another form of a written update, meet them for coffee if you can, or if not, at least make a phone call to give them an update. Doing so will help satisfy their need for a connection.

POWERS

Check items off the list. Powers want regular updates showing something they can cross off their checklist. The details are not as important as keeping them posted about whether or not you are on target in terms of timing. If you need something from a Power, be sure to specify that in your updates because Powers are so busy they will often miss follow-up if it is not called out specifically.

AUTHORITIES

Send detailed updates along the way. Authorities are the most concerned with project updates of all the Styles. And unlike with Controls, details are important to Authorities! Don't send high-level updates and expect an Authority to be satisfied. Instead, send in your detailed updates on time (hitting your deadline) or even early. That will demonstrate competence at managing a project. On the other hand, if an Authority is chasing you to get a project update, that's bad news—it means you are losing identity with them, and they will be more upset than you might think.

HOW TO HELP AN AUTHORITY FEEL COMFORTABLE ANSWERING YOUR QUESTIONS

"As an Authority, I would love it if people asked me questions with enough context and time to allow me to respond appropriately. It's very important for me to be seen as competent, knowing what I'm talking about. Quite often, that will require that I ask a few questions before I can provide a well-considered response, so I really appreciate it when people give me the space to be able to do that. I can't really answer a question without some context, because I really don't know what people are looking for otherwise. That's really how others can treat me according to the Diamond Rule, give me the information I need to make an educated decision or take an educated action. The keyword is educated. I need to be educated."

3. Knowing What To Do if a Breakdown Occurs

Even with the best of intentions and perfect planning, you know that you can't avoid every challenge and obstacle, so knowing how to recover successfully with each of the Styles when the inevitable happens is great preparation.

CONTROLS

Inevitably, all projects have breakdowns. When breakdowns do happen around a Control, their Survival Strategy of Dictate can come into play and you should be prepared for them to come across to you as arrogant. They will be thinking: "How could you have screwed up my idea?!" In order to help a Control get back on track, it will be critical for you to reconnect them to the big picture. If a Control has lost sight of their big picture, they will become very difficult to work with.

INFLUENCES

When something breaks down with an Influence, be prepared for them to become impatient. They will just want the issue to go away so they can move on. Due to their sincerity base to trust, it is important to handle the breakdown with a more personal touch—maybe an in-person meeting at a coffee shop and/ or maybe by starting with an apology, if it is warranted. Also important in this process is to allow an Influence to vent during a breakdown, because many times they learn through that venting process.

HOW TO BUILD STRONG IDENTITY WITH AN INFLUENCE

"As an Influence, an approach that works great with me is just to check on me for no reason other than to check on me. Just call me or show up without an agenda, I have no problem being interrupted, really. You don't need to reach out to me because something is wrong or there's a problem or even because you have new information I might find valuable or interesting. Those reasons are fine, but when somebody calls me and says, 'Hey, we haven't seen each other in a while, let's grab drinks or dinner,' that's how others can treat me like I want to be treated and make me feel good about the relationship."

POWERS

When something does breakdown with a Power, be on the look-out for them to show frustration—like asking "Why are all of these things in the way of getting this project done?" To help a Power get back on track, it is important to remember that they have a sincerity base to trust and would appreciate you working collaboratively with them to solve the issue. It is especially helpful to review priorities as sometimes Powers try to do everything at once when there is a breakdown. They forget that some things are always more important than other things on a project.

AUTHORITIES

When something does break down with an Authority, be on the lookout for them to be indifferent and defensive—wanting to protect themselves from looking like they did anything wrong, which primarily has to do (yet again) with their competence base to trust. To help an Authority get back on track, it is useful to leave them alone for a time and let them process (remember, they have the Hibernate Survival Strategy), but then you need to get them talking and get them to download their assessments about what happened. This is an opportunity for them to demonstrate their own competence. Definitely take notes and listen, and then make promises to fix the relevant issues they discuss.

MOVING AN AUTHORITY TO A DECISION BY BEING WILLING TO WALK AWAY

"One sale I recently made was with a classic Authority. I say classic because she would never make a decision,

Continued...

just keep asking more questions. I found it exasperating. Each time I answered one of her questions, it just created more questions for her. I finally went over to her office and sat down with a list of the last several rounds of questions she'd asked about. I read them off to her one-at-a-time, going down the list, checking off each item, demonstrating that I've provided her everything she had asked for. 'You wanted to know this, I provided you with this,' very specifically like that. At that point, I used the Diamond Rule to guide my next steps and said to her, 'You've had a lot of questions that we've worked hard to address. We're at a point now where we need to make decisions. To be clear, I want to work for you, but we need to be honest if we're going to work together or not. It's okay if you want to go a different direction if that's what needs to happen. I believe that I've outlined everything that we can do for you and that you have all the information you need to make a decision. So, if I have not provided you with what you need, then I haven't done a good job, and we should just shake hands and go our separate ways.' As soon as I expressed that I was willing to walk away, I got the business."

You've delivered and done a good job of managing the client. But wait, there's more! In the next chapter, we'll share the most effective ways to recognize the success of your work with your client.

CHAPTER 19

ACKNOWLEDGING SUCCESS

"No one who achieves success does so without acknowledging the help of others. The wise and confident acknowledge this help with gratitude."

— Alfred North Whitehead

Y ou know that a well-delivered acknowledgment or praise can go a long way for your clients. Who doesn't want positive things about them reflected back to them? But, as you've learned repeatedly throughout this book, a one-size-fits-all approach to anything doesn't really work. So, here's some Diamond Rule advice on how to best acknowledge and recognize success for a project for each of the Styles so that they feel truly valued:

CONTROLS

Acknowledge their idea. As we know, a Control has a competence base to trust, so an emotional acknowledgment is not necessarily the correct approach. Instead, consider how you might recognize them for their idea or even the legacy that will come from the project. This will speak to them more because of their underlying drive to create the future through a well-thought-out strategy.

INFLUENCES

Acknowledge the relationship. With their primary trust concern for sincerity, acknowledgment for an Influence needs to be more around the working relationship itself. Focusing on the professional friendship and how rewarding it was to work together will go much further than focusing on just the result of the project itself.

POWERS

Acknowledge their hard work. This works well for a Power and their sincerity base to trust. This means that their acknowledgment needs to be more personal in nature, and it should center around effort and results—how hard they worked on the project and what terrific results were achieved.

HOW A POWER LIKES TO
BE RECOGNIZED

"As a Power, I would like to be appreciated for all the work that I put into something and all the planning I did to get us there. If I executed and implemented well, I want to know that others know that. When someone appreciates something that I've worked on, like a plan or a deliverable, that really goes a long way for me. That's even better than someone acknowledging me directly. In fact, I'd rather it be about my work product than me. I'm proud to show off my checklists and spreadsheets and highlights and checkmarks. I'd almost do those things for free at some level because I just love to do that stuff."

AUTHORITIES

Acknowledge what you learned. An Authority, like a Control, approaches trust from a competence base, so their acknowledgment needs to be more professional in nature and focused on how much value their analytics brought to the project. Being acknowledged for how their perspective saved the team time and money is the sweet spot for an Authority.

Congratulations, you are now a Diamond Rule rockstar! You've successfully managed your client engagement right from the start. You've set your own concerns aside to build trust, develop a great rapport, learn what's most important to them, and taken a focused approach to work successfully with them every step of the way. Everyone feels great now at the end of the project, so like a good salesperson or client manager, you're thinking about what's next and how to get the next engagement going, which is exactly where we're headed in the next chapter!

CHAPTER 20

SETTING UP FOR THE NEXT GO-AROUND

"When a salesperson truly cares about you, trust forms,
and you're more likely to buy, come back for repeat
business, and refer new customers."

— Adam Grant

I t can be surprising at first, but the end of a project is the perfect time to solidify your relationship with your client. And,
just as you've learned every step of the way, taking a one-size-
fits-all approach is a dangerous play considering that all Styles
want to be treated differently.

This means it is time to apply the Diamond Rule! And, to that end,
here are a couple of actions for you to take that will help you strength-
en your relationship with your client once a project is completed:

1. Post-Project Focus

2. Going the Extra Mile

When you manage this transition well from end of previous project
to beginning of new one, you are leveraging all the goodwill and
effort extended so far, which makes the next round a much easier
and efficient use of time.

1. Post-Project Focus

Your client may not be thinking about their next project just yet, but
it is always most effective to strike while the iron's hot. Here are the
various approaches to take to be successful with the different Styles:

CONTROLS

Focus on what comes next. Unlike an Authority, a Control does not
tend to appreciate a post-project retrospective. Furthermore, they
are not as interested in celebrations as a Power or an Influence.
Instead, a follow-up meeting in their office to go over their view of
the next idea is a great way to further connect with a Control.

INFLUENCES

Celebrate! An Influence likes to celebrate with something social
following a successful project. Whether it's a lunch, a dinner, a

game of tennis, or a round of golf, Influences enjoy a one-on-one experience to help them feel even more connected for a future project.

POWERS

Ask about the next item on their list. A Power is production-oriented, and they always have a next item on their to-do list. Asking a Power to go over the next item and to share with you how you can help them is a great way to demonstrate your loyalty and your commitment to their future.

AUTHORITIES

Offer to do a project retrospective. Due to the fact that an Authority has a primary time frame of the past, the best offer you can make is to do a project retrospective and evaluate what worked and what didn't work. Even if an Authority declines the offer, they will appreciate the fact that you are committed to learning from the past. Chances are, however, they won't decline the offer!

2. Going the Extra Mile

As the expression goes, this action truly separates you from your competition. In the words of NFL Hall of Fame quarterback Roger Staubach, "There are no traffic jams along the extra mile." Going the extra mile means that you are providing something beyond what people are expecting, something they haven't considered, something that will both surprise and delight them. This is the spirit of lagniappe. Lagniappe is a Creole word for "a little something extra." Mark Twain once called it, "A word worth traveling to New Orleans to get." It's that extra effort to go beyond the transaction to honor the relationship. Going the extra mile is the central tenet in the Goldfish book series and a key driver of differentiation.

Let's look at how to deliver that little extra with each of the four Styles:

CONTROLS

Due to the fact that a Control sometimes struggles with the relationships around them and building morale, one thing you can do to go the extra mile is acknowledge their team. The key, of course, is that their team must have earned the accolades. Assuming this to be true, there are two outcomes for a Control:

- The Control does not necessarily need to make the acknowledgment because you have stepped into a relationship role and are making the acknowledgment on their behalf.

- The Control can feel competent having put the team together—something that enhances their image.

In the end, taking these "extra" actions is a powerful way to strengthen your relationship with a Control once a project is over. It will also help you build a lasting identity as someone who sees the value of a well-thought-out strategy and who is aligned with them on their future.

INFLUENCES

The one thing that you should know about Influences now is that they like to have fun and they want to have fun with you. So, to really connect with your Influence client, there are two primary ways of going the extra mile:

- Plan a celebration that includes others who worked on the project, and then shine the spotlight on the Influence at some point during the celebration.

- Present the Influence with a nice plaque (or other notice of achievement) that they can proudly display in their office.

The key element of success in both approaches here is that there is a celebration of their contribution *in front of others.*

Taking these actions after a successful project is a phenomenal way to strengthen the relationship with an Influence and build a lasting identity with them, because you have demonstrated you are someone who values relationships and are fun to work with.

POWERS

A Power often likes to have some type of a celebration as their extra mile. However, if you are going to do it (for example, a celebratory dinner), you need to make sure to make the invitation for others on their team as well. Powers are inclusive and would rather have a team celebration than a one-on-one celebration.

AUTHORITIES

An Authority tends not to be focused on celebrating a project's success, which can be difficult for Influences especially. Instead, the opportunity for the extra mile with an Authority is to get them a gift certificate (free money!) which enables them to research how they want to spend it—it could take them months due to their Hibernate Survival Strategy!

Setting up the next go-around with each of the Behavioral Styles—by solidifying your post-project focus and going above and beyond—is an excellent way to strategically strengthen your relationship once a project is over. This will also help you build a lasting identity as someone who is a competent partner, who is committed to learning, and who goes the extra mile for those around you.

CHAPTER 21

DIAMOND RULE MATRIX

"I know you're out there. I can feel you now. I know that you're afraid... you're afraid of change. I don't know the future. I didn't come here to tell you how this is going to end. I came here to tell you how it's going to begin."

— Neo from the movie "The Matrix"

The Diamond Rule Matrix provides an "at a glance reference tool" for each style.

HOW TO USE THE MATRIX:

Find your style across the top. Then scroll down to find the style of the person you are selling. Within each box, you'll find tips on how to put the Diamond Rule into action.

YOUR STYLE

THEIR STYLE	DIAMOND APPROACH	CONTROL
CONTROL	*MANAGE YOUR BIOLOGY*	***MINDSET:*** *Think more about how to help them* ***NEUTRALIZE:*** *Don't fight their ideas*
CONTROL	*EMPATHIZE WITH THEM*	**FOUNDATION:** Prepare to be a Power **FIRST MEETING:** Let them drive **NEGOTIATING:** Tie outcomes to their ideas **ACKNOWLEDGING:** Great idea! **FOLLOWING UP:** Your team was outstanding!
INFLUENCE	*MANAGE YOUR BIOLOGY*	***MINDSET:*** *Focus on being more personable* ***NEUTRALIZE:*** *Being too direct or pushy*
INFLUENCE	*EMPATHIZE WITH THEM*	**FOUNDATION:** Focus on sincerity vs. competence **FIRST MEETING:** Discuss people they know **NEGOTIATING:** Listen and make process **ACKNOWLEDGING:** Enjoyed working with you! **FOLLOWING UP:** Let's meet up for lunch
POWER	*MANAGE YOUR BIOLOGY*	***MINDSET:*** *Zero in on tactics and be pragmatic* ***NEUTRALIZE:*** *Focusing only on big picture*
POWER	*EMPATHIZE WITH THEM*	**FOUNDATION:** Be cordial and avoid being pushy **FIRST MEETING:** Come across as a hard worker **NEGOTIATING:** Be collaborative not just 1-sided **ACKNOWLEDGING:** We make a great team! **FOLLOWING UP:** What can I do next for you?
AUTHORITY	*MANAGE YOUR BIOLOGY*	***MINDSET:*** *Be interested in historical context* ***NEUTRALIZE:*** *Talking too much about the future*
AUTHORITY	*EMPATHIZE WITH THEM*	**FOUNDATION:** Prepare to listen to their concerns **FIRST MEETING:** Let them discuss obstacles **NEGOTIATING:** Slow down & talk through points **ACKNOWLEDGING:** Your insights were a lifesaver! **FOLLOWING UP:** Let's do a project retrospective

YOUR STYLE

DIAMOND APPROACH		INFLUENCE
CONTROL	MANAGE YOUR BIOLOGY	**MINDSET:** Be on point & more business focused **NEUTRALIZE:** Instinct to "just wing it"
	EMPATHIZE WITH THEM	**FOUNDATION:** Prepare with crisp approach **FIRST MEETING:** Focus on their business point **NEGOTIATING:** Be more formal than informal **ACKNOWLEDGING:** Great strategy for us to follow! **FOLLOWING UP:** Where's the next challenge?
INFLUENCE	MANAGE YOUR BIOLOGY	**MINDSET:** Be social AND help with structure **NEUTRALIZE:** Temptation not to do business
	EMPATHIZE WITH THEM	**FOUNDATION:** Don't just create a friend **FIRST MEETING:** Have fun but don't compete **NEGOTIATING:** Keep it light, but capture details **ACKNOWLEDGING:** Let's go celebrate! **FOLLOWING UP:** Let's have some more fun
POWER	MANAGE YOUR BIOLOGY	**MINDSET:** Avoid being unorganized **NEUTRALIZE:** Over-emphasis on sincerity
	EMPATHIZE WITH THEM	**FOUNDATION:** Prepare to be more like a Power **FIRST MEETING:** Get invested in their projects **NEGOTIATING:** Go point by point, work together **ACKNOWLEDGING:** I love working with you! **FOLLOWING UP:** How can I help you further?
AUTHORITY	MANAGE YOUR BIOLOGY	**MINDSET:** One thought and one step at a time **NEUTRALIZE:** Careful not to come across chaotic
	EMPATHIZE WITH THEM	**FOUNDATION:** Act more like an Authority **FIRST MEETING:** Be patient, listen, & don't just talk **NEGOTIATING:** Have grounding for your positions **ACKNOWLEDGING:** Thank you for having my back! **FOLLOWING UP:** Here's a gift certificate for you

THEIR STYLE

YOUR STYLE

THEIR STYLE	DIAMOND APPROACH	POWER
CONTROL	*MANAGE YOUR BIOLOGY*	**MINDSET**: *Be organized and focused on priorities* **NEUTRALIZE**: *Coming across as too busy to implement*
	EMPATHIZE WITH THEM	**FOUNDATION**: Focus on high level objectives, not tactics **FIRST MEETING**: Show ability to think strategically **NEGOTIATING**: Appeal to their image throughout **ACKNOWLEDGING**: Your direction kept me on point! **FOLLOWING UP**: What is the next mountain to climb?
INFLUENCE	*MANAGE YOUR BIOLOGY*	**MINDSET**: *Be open to brainstorming* **NEUTRALIZE**: *Need to leave with a checklist too quickly*
	EMPATHIZE WITH THEM	**FOUNDATION**: Relax at the beginning & bring structure **FIRST MEETING**: Don't impose too much structure **NEGOTIATING**: Be patient, let them go first **ACKNOWLEDGING**: I appreciated your high energy! **FOLLOWING UP**: Here's a plaque for your great work
POWER	*MANAGE YOUR BIOLOGY*	**MINDSET**: *Create a partner and focus on being a Control* **NEUTRALIZE**: *Temptation of only focusing tactically*
	EMPATHIZE WITH THEM	**FOUNDATION**: Show loyalty early and often **FIRST MEETING**: Compare lists and adhere to theirs **NEGOTIATING**: Work toward a presumptive next step **ACKNOWLEDGING**: We are a powehouse team! **FOLLOWING UP**: What's our next to-do together?
AUTHORITY	*MANAGE YOUR BIOLOGY*	**MINDSET**: *Focus on quality over volume* **NEUTRALIZE**: *Rushing any one direction without thinking*
	EMPATHIZE WITH THEM	**FOUNDATION**: Prepare your resume and credentials **FIRST MEETING**: Show you are thinking about priorities **NEGOTIATING**: Be exacting & focus on quality over cost **ACKNOWLEDGING**: I appreciate your detailed approach! **FOLLOWING UP**: Here are my thoughts on what worked

YOUR STYLE

DIAMOND APPROACH		AUTHORITY
THEIR STYLE — **CONTROL**	*MANAGE YOUR BIOLOGY*	**MINDSET**: *Be open to new ideas and new possibilites* **NEUTRALIZE**: *Too much focus on reasons why not*
	EMPATHIZE WITH THEM	**FOUNDATION**: Demonstrate you get their ideas **FIRST MEETING**: Be interested in their love for the future **NEGOTIATING**: Be passionate in the process **ACKNOWLEDGING**: You showed me what's possible! **FOLLOWING UP**: Can we brainstorm about the future?
INFLUENCE	*MANAGE YOUR BIOLOGY*	**MINDSET**: *Be authentically interested in them* **NEUTRALIZE**: *Focus on numbers and details*
	EMPATHIZE WITH THEM	**FOUNDATION**: Prepare to go faster than feels natural **FIRST MEETING**: Avoid slowing down their process **NEGOTIATING**: Don't argue all points, pick your battles **ACKNOWLEDGING**: You made this project fun! **FOLLOWING UP**: Can I buy you dinner?
POWER	*MANAGE YOUR BIOLOGY*	**MINDSET**: *Bring a bias for action & getting down to business* **NEUTRALIZE**: *Coming across as negative on past work*
	EMPATHIZE WITH THEM	**FOUNDATION**: Create a checklist of discussion topics **FIRST MEETING**: Move with pace over precision focus **NEGOTIATING**: Avoid being rude or pushy **ACKNOWLEDGING**: You've done great work! **FOLLOWING UP**: Can we do more great work together?
AUTHORITY	*MANAGE YOUR BIOLOGY*	**MINDSET**: *Discuss the past but focus on the future* **NEUTRALIZE**: *Comfort level of not making an decisions*
	EMPATHIZE WITH THEM	**FOUNDATION**: Avoid analysis paralysis **FIRST MEETING**: Let them talk, then act like a Control **NEGOTIATING**: Don't wait forever; walk away if need be **ACKNOWLEDGING**: Your analysis was key at every step! **FOLLOWING UP**: I created this deal review for you

Now, let's finish up by looking at five big takeaways.

SECTION IV

CLOSING

CHAPTER 22

TOP FIVE TAKEAWAYS

"Great advice is like aspirin ... it only works
if you take it."

— Dave Murphy

Here are the top five takeaways from *Diamond Goldfish*:

1. EVOLVE TO THE DIAMOND RULE

The Diamond Rule symbolizes the best future approach to achieving prosperity in business. It's the next evolution of managing relationships and winning in the 4.0 version of business. Let's review the previous versions:

- 1.0 is the Silver Rule to "do no harm."

- 2.0 is the Golden Rule "treating others the way you would like to be treated."

- 3.0 is the Platinum Rule "treating others the way that they want to be treated."

The Diamond Rule, the 4.0 version of business, is "the practice of managing yourself under pressure and addressing the needs of others to avoid their triggers."

2. HONOR YOUR BIOLOGY AND REWIRE IT

We like to think of ourselves as advanced beings living in a modern world. But, as it turns out, we are still operating on fairly primitive biology. And under pressure, that biology predictably triggers your hard-wired survival instincts every time it detects a threat. When you're exposed to a high enough level of pressure, for instance when you find yourself in a tense negotiation with a client, your brain loses its ability to distinguish between actual and perceived risk. The good news is that even though these pathways are hard-wired into your brain, you actually have the ability to lay new pathways over the top of the old ones, altering your behavior. In other words, while your amygdala has no reasoning, it can be reasoned with—you can teach your amygdala not to activate under identity pressure. You need to learn how to manage your own behavior under pressure.

3. KNOW YOUR STYLE

Knowing your own style is the price of admission if you want to succeed in the game of business. If you know what your style is, you can begin applying the Diamond Rule to your relationships. The key is to understand your tendencies. When we are under pressure, we are prone to acting very much like reptiles or animals. This chart explains our behavior under pressure and holds the keys to the four styles:

BIOLOGY	NEOCORTEX CONCERN	NEED TO KNOW...	BEHAVIORAL STYLE
DICTATE	Certainty	There is a plan	Control (Casey)
MIGRATE	Freedom	There are options and flexibility	Influence (Izzy)
TOLERATE	Stability	There is a structure	Power (Peyton)
HIBERNATE	Security	How things will ultimately work out	Authority (Avery)

4. M.I.N.E. FOR DIAMONDS

Here are the four questions when mining for Diamonds:

[Mindset] What Style am I dealing with?

[Identify] What is the situation?

[Neutralize] What do I need to do to set aside my Style? Before you will ever be able to relate better with others, it's important to look in the mirror and neutralize

your own reactions to pressure. The dictionary definition of neutralize is "to render (something) harmless
by applying an opposite force or effect."

[Empathize] What am I doing to address their needs?
Being empathetic means increasing your focus on the
concerns of others. When you learn what causes other
people to feel stress, you can help reduce their pressure
and instantly improve your identity along the way.

5. THE THREE KEYS TO SUCCESS

There are only three ways to achieve success with the Diamond
Rule—APPLY, APPLY, and APPLY. In the words of Rob Hill, Sr.
"Knowledge without application is a waste. Those who just "know"
will always come in second to those who "do." Put what you know
in motion . . . apply what you've learned."

We hope you've enjoyed the book and that you will achieve prosperity from practicing the Diamond Rule. Here's how you can help
us create more prosperity with Diamond Goldfish thinkers:

- Apply what you've learned in this book to build better
  relationships

- Share the book with others

- Bring us in to speak at your conference

- Book us for a workshop or training session

- Connect with us on LinkedIn

ABOUT THE AUTHORS

STAN PHELPS

Stan Phelps is a best-selling author, keynote speaker, and workshop facilitator. He believes that today's organizations must focus on meaningful differentiation to win the hearts of both employees and customers.

He is the founder of PurpleGoldfish.com. Purple Goldfish is a think tank of customer experience and employee engagement experts that offers keynotes and workshops that drive loyalty and sales. The group helps organizations connect with the hearts and minds of customers and employees.

Prior to PurpleGoldfish.com, Stan had a 20-year career in marketing that included leadership positions at IMG, adidas, PGA Exhibitions, and Synergy. At Synergy, he worked on award-winning experiential programs for top brands such as KFC, Wachovia, NASCAR, Starbucks, and M&M's.

Stan is a TEDx speaker, a Forbes contributor, and a Certified Speaking Professional. His writing is syndicated on top sites such as Customer Think and Business2Community. He has spoken at more than 400 events across Australia, Bahrain, Canada, Ecuador, France, Germany, Holland, Israel, Japan, Malaysia, Peru, Russia, Singapore, Spain, Sweden, the UK, and the US.

He is the author of 11 other business books:

Purple Goldfish 2.0 - 10 Ways to Attract Raving Customers
Green Goldfish 2.0 - 15 Keys to Driving Employee Engagement

Golden Goldfish - The Vital Few

Blue Goldfish - Using Technology, Data, and Analytics to Drive Both Profits and Prophets

Purple Goldfish Service Edition - 12 Ways Hotels, Restaurants, and Airlines Win the Right Customers

Red Goldfish - Motivating Sales and Loyalty Through Shared Passion and Purpose

Pink Goldfish - Defy Normal, Exploit Imperfection, and Captivate Your Customers

Purple Goldfish Franchise Edition - The Ultimate S.Y.S.T.E.M. for Franchisors and Franchisees

Yellow Goldfish - Nine Ways to Drive Happiness in Business for Growth, Productivity, and Prosperity

Gray Goldfish - Navigating the Gray Areas to Successfully Lead Every Generation

Red Goldfish Nonprofit Edition - How the Best Nonprofits Leverage Their Purpose to Increase Engagement and Impact

and one fun one...
Bar Tricks, Bad Jokes, & Even Worse Stories

Stan received a BS in Marketing and Human Resources from Marist College, a JD/MBA from Villanova University, and a certificate for Achieving Breakthrough Service from Harvard Business School. He is a Certified Net Promoter Associate and has taught as an adjunct professor at NYU, Rutgers University, and Manhattanville College.

Stan is also a fellow at Maddock Douglas, an innovation consulting firm in Chicago. Stan lives in Cary, North Carolina, with his wife, Jennifer, and their two boys, Thomas and James.

To book Stan for an upcoming keynote, webinar, or workshop go to stanphelpsspeaks.com. You can reach Stan at stan@purple-goldfish.com or call +1.919.360.4702 or follow him on Twitter: @StanPhelpsPG.

TRAVIS CARSON

Travis is the driving force behind Market Force, having lived, used, taught, and coached its principle practices for over 20 years. Travis is a highly sought-after presenter, coach, and trainer. Travis's clients think of him as their "Economic Chief of Staff."

A life-long learner and entrepreneur, Travis has employed the value of Market Force's Human Performance Technology to help run his own businesses as well as to coach hundreds of others. Travis has played business leadership roles in several companies ranging from home health care to energy-efficient lighting to real estate investment. Each of these businesses experienced solid growth and performance under Travis's leadership. It is through these experiences that he has been able to fine tune the Market Force system and help his clients extract the maximum value out of the program.

Travis has executive consulting experience with companies spanning more than 20 different industries, ranging in size from start-up to multi-national. With his combination of real-time operations and business ownership experience plus graduate-level education in law and business, Travis provides business leaders with tools and perspective for solving their most difficult business issues.

Travis earned both his MBA and his JD from the University of Arizona. He was a four-time nationally ranked tennis player and a seven-time nationally ranked triathlete as well as a three-time Ironman Triathlon finisher. Travis and his wife, Alison, live in Tucson, Arizona, with their four children.

TONY COOPER

As Market Force's CEO, Tony is passionate about spreading its powerful human dynamics methodology around the world. As a serial entrepreneur, Tony learned first-hand how easy it is for people to get in their own way. He spent many years developing innovative strategies for clients, only to see many of them fall short of their goals and aspirations due to the ineffective way that people unconsciously interact with each other at work. When he discovered the Market Force methodology for elevating human performance in the workplace, he knew he had found the true path for upgrading humanware at work by helping people overcome their detrimental biological instincts.

Tony is a personal growth junkie and loves instigating true breakthroughs for others through his fascination of playing the "game behind the game." He is passionate about the entrepreneurial spirit and he brings out the best in others by helping them simplify complicated issues and supporting them to gain new skills and insights quickly.

Driven by innovation in service of humanity, Tony spent the early part of his career in the Detroit automotive industry, as a Silicon Valley product design consultant, and as the leader of a nationally-acclaimed, high-end, contemporary furniture business. Since that time, he has played strategic leadership roles in several groundbreaking coaching and training businesses.

Tony graduated with distinction as a mechanical engineer from Cornell University. He prioritizes giving back to society as a volunteer mediator and through his strategic volunteer contributions with powerful, community-based organizations. In his youth, his idol was industrial design revolutionary, Raymond Loewy. He was also a nationally-ranked springboard diver and competitive Tae Kwon Do martial artist. His greatest joys are snowboarding, scuba diving and spending quality time with his family outside of Sacramento, California.

To discuss Market Force training for your company or to have Travis or Tony deliver a keynote or workshop, please go to www.marketforceglobal.com. You can reach Travis at tcarson@marketforceglobal.com or +1.520.631.8395. You can reach Tony at tcooper@marketforceglobal.com or +1.415.748.2213.

OTHER COLORS IN THE GOLDFISH SERIES

PURPLE GOLDFISH 2.0 – 10 WAYS TO ATTRACT RAVING CUSTOMERS

Purple Goldfish is based on the Purple Goldfish Project, a crowd-sourcing effort that collected more than 1,001 examples of signa-ture-added value. The book draws inspiration from the concept of lagniappe, providing 10 practical strategies for winning the hearts of customers and influencing positive word of mouth.

GREEN GOLDFISH 2.0 – 15 KEYS TO DRIVING EMPLOYEE ENGAGEMENT

Green Goldfish is based on the simple premise that "happy engaged employees create happy enthused customers." The book focuses on 15 different ways to drive employee engagement and reinforce a strong corporate culture.

GOLDEN GOLDFISH – THE VITAL FEW

Golden Goldfish examines the importance of your top 20 percent of customers and employees. The book showcases nine ways to drive loyalty and retention with these two critical groups.

BLUE GOLDFISH - USING TECHNOLOGY, DATA, AND ANA-LYTICS TO DRIVE BOTH PROFITS AND PROPHETS

Blue Goldfish examines how to leverage technology, data, and ana-lytics to do a "little something extra" to improve the experience for the customer. The book is based on a collection of over 300 case studies. It examines the three R's: Relationship, Responsiveness, and Readiness. *Blue Goldfish* uncovers eight different ways to turn insights into action.

RED GOLDFISH - MOTIVATING SALES AND LOYALTY THROUGH SHARED PASSION AND PURPOSE

Purpose is changing the way we work and how customers choose business partners. It is driving loyalty, and it's on its way to becoming the ultimate differentiator in business. *Red Goldfish* shares cutting edge examples and reveals the eight ways businesses can embrace purpose that drives employee engagement, fuels the bottom line, and makes an impact on the lives of those it serves.

PURPLE GOLDFISH SERVICE EDITION - 12 WAYS HOTELS, RESTAURANTS, AND AIRLINES WIN THE RIGHT CUSTOMERS

Purple Goldfish Service Edition is about differentiation via added value and marketing to your existing customers via G.L.U.E. (**g**iving **l**ittle **u**nexpected **e**xtras). Packed with over 100 examples, the book focuses on the 12 ways to do the "little extras" to improve the customer experience for restaurants, hotels, and airlines. The end result is increased sales, happier customers, and positive word of mouth.

PINK GOLDFISH - DEFY NORMAL, EXPLOIT IMPERFECTION, AND CAPTIVATE YOUR CUSTOMERS

Companies need to stand out in a crowded marketplace, but true differentiation is increasingly rare. Based on over 250 case studies, *Pink Goldfish* provides an unconventional seven-part framework for achieving competitive separation by embracing flaws instead of fixing them.

PURPLE GOLDFISH FRANCHISE EDITION - THE ULTIMATE S.Y.S.T.E.M. FOR FRANCHISORS AND FRANCHISEES

Packed with over 100 best-practice examples, *Purple Goldfish Franchise Edition* focuses on the six keys to creating a successful franchise S.Y.S.T.E.M. and a dozen ways to create a signature customer experience.

YELLOW GOLDFISH - NINE WAYS TO DRIVE HAPPINESS IN BUSINESS FOR GROWTH, PRODUCTIVITY, AND PROSPERITY

There should be only one success metric in business and that's happiness. A Yellow Goldfish is any time a business does a little extra to contribute to the happiness of its customers, employees, or society. Based on nearly 300 case studies, *Yellow Goldfish* provides a nine-part framework for happiness-driven growth, productivity, and prosperity in business.

GRAY GOLDFISH - NAVIGATING THE GRAY AREAS TO SUCCESSFULLY LEAD EVERY GENERATION

How do you successfully lead the five generations in today's workforce? You need tools to navigate. Filled with over 100 case studies and the Generational Matrix, *Gray Goldfish* provides the definitive map for leaders to follow as they recruit, train, manage, and inspire across the generations.

RED GOLDFISH NONPROFIT EDITION – HOW THE BEST NONPROFITS LEVERAGE THEIR PURPOSE TO INCREASE ENGAGEMENT AND IMPACT

The competition is fierce in the nonprofit world, even when competing in different spaces. *Red Goldfish Nonprofit Edition* explores the signature ways nonprofits reinforce their purpose and stand out in a crowded marketplace, whether it is an extra level of recognition for key donors, a special incentive designed to keep their best employees, or something simple like a luncheon to recognize volunteers or highest fundraisers. If you work at a nonprofit, this book will help you deliver "a little extra" to your stakeholders.

PN3FM8YK

Made in the USA
Middletown, DE
18 February 2020

84957632R10166